It's all Sales

It's people's business

Original title: Verkopen doe je altijd, mensen kopen van mensen
Translation: Marieke Klaver for 'Good Luck English Language Productions, the Netherlands
Cover design: Robyright, The Netherlands
Layout design: Wizard Wise, The Netherlands
Publisher: Wizard Wise, The Netherlands
Distibutor: Lulu.com
ISBN: 978-94-90520-02-1

www.itsallsales.com

It's all Sales

It's people's business

Dick Tol

Wim Bouman

Preface

Dick Tol started writing down his experiences because his friend Wim Bouman noticed the benefits that could be derived by others from Dick's experiences. Given Wim's background in Sales it was no surprise that he was able to draw an analogy between Dick's experiences and selling. That is why Wim analyzed every story and added useful theoretical background information and relevant tools for those who are interested in sales and who are also convinced that 'people buy from people'. It is also relevant to those interested in real-life experiences, for they will find stories they can relate to and may even benefit from in a business setting but also in their private lives.

The story so far...

Dick Tol grew up in a small village in the Netherlands. The family home was a warm and happy one with his father trying to make a living as a building contractor. Dick did well in school but conscription thwarted his initial ambition to become a doctor. He then discovers a whole new world when he is hired by a bank and employed in the automation department. Although when Dick first gets hired automation is still in its infancy, he immediately recognizes the tremendous impact automation will have on the future of banking and he embraces the new technology wholeheartedly. His ambition is fairly straightforward at first for he intends to become a computer programmer. In order to reach this goal he needs to attend evening classes for five years in addition to his demanding job. His career takes off and he is offered an increasing amount of responsibility. Challenges like having to write business plans without any previous experience or becoming responsible for recruitment he takes in his stride and in doing so he learns many a valuable lesson. There is one aspect, however, he cannot not control and that is company politics. Although he does not want to get involved he tries to keep abreast of what is going on and in particular when it involved his staff and colleagues. Will he manage to stay clear from company politics and remain neutral or will he have to get involved in order to protect his staff and colleagues, especially because many of them have become friends over the years.

Next to the professional development of a successful bank director the book also offers an interesting insight in the development of banking automation. Nowadays it is hard to imagine the times when we did not have access to cash points (ATMs) and electronic payment but from Dick's story it becomes clear that many battles had to be fought before consumers could have access to 24/7 banking. Yet, a new challenge presents itself to Dick and his company: the introduction of the single currency (Euro).

Still, perhaps the most valuable lessons he learns are those on a personal level. When it comes to his career he works hard and is a fast learner and above all, he learns to trust his intuition. Yet while his career skyrockets he feels that his personal life is falling apart. When he first got married he lived in a council house and together they had to work hard to earn enough to buy the basics. But now that he is financially secure he finds it increasingly difficult to create a warm home for his wife and beloved daughter.

He realizes that over the years he and his wife have drifted apart and that he can no longer communicate with her. His wife at the same time tries to come to terms with an unhappy childhood and attempts to find refuge in alcohol. While Dick tries to protect his daughter from the drink-induced aggressive outbursts from her mother he bears the brunt of her attacks. Also in this case Dick does not want to give up. When he took his wedding vows he promised to take care of his wife no matter what. He feels responsible for her well being and even though he feels miserable he wants to stand by her as she is trying to come to terms with her past. Eventually Dick has to accept that he is as human as the next man when during a horrible confrontation he hits back his drunk wife.

What keeps him going is the fact that he has been able to communicate with a spiritual presence he refers to as 'My God'. Being disappointed in traditional religions he gratefully allows this presence into his life. Whenever he is in doubt or has a difficult decision to take he is always able to find a quiet moment in which to ask his God for help.

Standard code of conduct for a salesperson

Some people say that they are born to sell. This is not necessarily true, because you can learn to sell. When it comes down to it, everyone is selling something to someone. Look at your own life and be aware that you learned to sell yourself as well. It already starts in infancy when you have fight for your position in the family. You do that by selling yourself and that continues in school, with your family, with friends, girl or boyfriend, the in-laws and at work with regard to your boss and colleagues. You are always selling.

Think about what you did as a salesperson with your hair, your clothes, the meeting etc. and assess your feelings. Were you nervous? Were you incoherent? Were you well prepared? Were you able to say everything you wanted? Did you listen properly? And did you reach your goal?

The above is a simple outline of the sales process. When you analyse the sales process, it all starts with good preparation, followed by the actual sales and finally the evaluation of the sales process. This process, in fact, comes naturally to people.

We can, however, learn about these sales processes from others. There are a number of rules we can learn which will always contribute to a successful and positive result. Perhaps you are already familiar with these rules but we will repeat them anyway.

1. Love people and enjoy dealing with them.
2. Be willing and able to communicate because no products were ever sold without communication.
3. Believe in the product or service that you offer. Speak realistically about the product or service you want to sell. Do not lie but there is no need to tell the whole truth.
4. Know your customer. There are many ways of gathering information and there is, of course, always the Internet.
5. Think positively.
6. Always be in a good mood, wear clean and decent clothes, keep your hair tidy and make sure there is no body odour. Also, dress for the occasion and the type of customer.
7. Make sure you possess some general knowledge of what is going on in the world and in particular in the customer's environment. The customer will appreciate it if you can talk to him about the latest developments. This knowledge may also be useful to break the ice.

8. Always treat your customer with respect. Listen carefully to what he has to say. Anticipate on his story and adapt your sales pitch accordingly when possible.
9. Try to make the occasional joke when dealing with a customer. Laughing is good for people's health; it makes people happy and puts them in a good mood. Cheerful and happy people are more likely to buy.
10. Always evaluate the visit afterwards. Keep in mind, though, that it does not matter what *you* thought of the conversation but that the customer's feelings are far more important. Try to find out.

Remember: People buy from People!

We all know the principle that you have to look at your own behaviour to understand that of others. Look at what you do when you buy something. Sometimes you can buy an item everywhere but you still go to the one shop where you like the service. One bad experience and you will never return. Think about other examples of your own buying behaviour.

It's all sales

Remember that in sales it is always important to determine what is important to your (prospective) customer. The rules given above are important but are useless unless you and your customer are not on the same wavelength. Be genuinely interested in your customer because he will know if you are not sincere. He will never say so, but the result is that he will not buy from you. And you? You will never find out why the deal went wrong and you will continue making the same mistakes. When it comes to selling it is not the product that you sell, but what the product or service will do for your customer.

Arguing for argument's sake

I had learned my lesson; at least I hoped I had. I was very careful next time around when I had to recruit a new Head of the Development and Maintenance Department. The appointment of the Head of the Information Centre was a success and he was a valued colleague. I asked him whether there were any former colleagues he could think of that would be interested in considering the position of Head Development and Maintenance in my department. A week later he told me he had found just the man for the position. The candidate was his best friend and they had been employed together by a large bank. I was pleased because it all sounded good and I thought I had solved a problem. Since the former Head of the Development and Maintenance left I had taken over his tasks and I could do with a bit of breathing space.

The newly appointed Head turned out to be a strange character. In every meeting he attended he opposed every single proposition. Not on paper beforehand but always verbally and during the meeting. He enjoyed endless discussions on just about every topic. When I asked him why he favoured lengthy discussions he answered that with his former employer (the large bank) they had trained him to encourage lengthy discussions for they believed it would lead to better alternatives. I told him in no uncertain terms that he had to change tactics. If he wanted discussions, he was to have them before the meeting and if he wanted to contribute something to the meeting he was to do so in writing so during the meeting it could be dealt with as a formality.

Another thing struck me. Contrary to the behaviour of the Head of the Information Centre, he was lazy. He told me over drinks once that he really did not like to work and that he would much rather have his wife working full-time so he could stay home. This attitude did not fit in with the rest of the department staff at all and small wonder it met with resistance from his colleagues.

He even managed to appoint two new colleagues who displayed the same type of behaviour and also did not fit in with the departmental culture. They displayed the same bad attitude towards work as their manager.

Apparently something had changed in his private life because after a couple of months he started to give of a sweaty smell. It was so bad that my secretary placed a toilet freshener on his desk hoping he would get the message. Unfortunately he did not.

Enough was enough. Once again I had appointed the wrong person and I was forced to take action. I discussed the matter with his friend, the Head of the

Information Centre. When I confronted him with his friend's behaviour he was quite surprised and promised to have a serious word with him.

A month later the Head of Development and Maintenance resigned unexpectedly. He wanted stay at home and devote his time to raising his daughter. His wife would take up a full-time position.

I learned that I had to go back to selecting my own management staff and had to trust my own intuition. Recruiting a suitable team member is not easy, though.

It's all sales

I am convinced that the best decisions are made when guided by intuition. Having said that, it is of course also important to have access to relevant data, figures and experience. Yet the final go or no go decision must be based on your instinct.

The supplier's budget

Basically my company's core business involved cash withdrawals and money exchange. We depended heavily on the number of tourists that were to visit the Netherlands during the holidays and festive season. The number of tourists would also depend on the weather forecast for the aforementioned holidays. Our company's policy was based on income derived from tourist transactions, which meant that after a successful Easter Holiday season I was allowed to make additional investments. A true shopkeeper's mentality.

Our main hardware supplier, the market leader, always had a budget campaign in March. New budgets as well as the sales targets for the coming year were set.

The Account Manager of this hardware supplier paid me a visit because she wished to determine how much we intended to invest in the company's hardware in the year to come. He required the information for the financial plan for the coming year. I told her I did not know, since our investments depended heavily on whether the tourist season was a success or not. She did not like the answer and left me, clearly disappointed. Later that day the Account Manager contacted my secretary to make an appointment for early the next morning. Apparently they were in a hurry.

I was slightly irritated by the behaviour and arrogance displayed by the hardware supplier. It seemed as if they wanted to extract promises from me I could not possibly keep. When the Account Manager and her Manager arrived the next morning I made them sit at my desk. I of course did not fail to mention the fact that I was busy preparing for the day's meetings and had little time to spare.

The manager confronted me straight away and told me it was a disgrace that I had refused to submit the desired figures. There was no stopping him until he had finished his story and it seemed as if he was on autocue. What it came down to was that I had to understand that they had to prepare a budget. As soon as he finished a silence descended upon the room.

I looked at him for quite a while and then asked him very politely whether he knew what the weather would be like coming Easter and whether he expected many tourists to visit the Netherlands. My question surprised him and he replied that he did not know. "Well, neither do I" I responded "and that's exactly the reason why I don't know whether we'll be investing in new hardware or not".

He looked at me and as if in a daze he left the office without saying goodbye, the Account Manager following in his tracks. That was the last thing I ever heard about the matter.

I learned that it is very difficult for a market leader to realise that 'customer is king'. This supplier became arrogant and thought they could determine what the customer needed and should do.

A good salesperson knows his place. When a strong company backs you, you will derive more mental strength from that fact than when your company is a less important player. However, when you talk to a customer you will have to earn his respect and this requires advanced communicative skills. Showing what you are worth and adopt an attitude of equality. That is how you will win the customer's respect. And a customer who respects you …

Innovation sells

In order to have all credit card transactions accepted by all our service desks and phone booths and for the processing of all banking transactions we had implemented in conjunction with a major Dutch Telecom Operator a 'Switch' computer. This 'Switch' computer had an online interface with the credit card companies for authorisation and validation of transactions.

At the same point in time the combined banks were working on implementing the same 'Switch' for the acceptance of direct debit card transactions at the retailer's shop counters. We did not want to wait for that to happen though, because the banks would not process credit card transactions.

The combined banks met with a lot of opposition from the retailers in the Netherlands. The argument mainly concentrated on the costs of direct debit card transactions. Who was going to pick up the bill? Originally the retailers were going to foot the bill but they thought the costs were insurmountable. The largest and most important retailer in the Netherlands refused to cooperate for that reason. The whole process had come to a standstill because of the arguments. According to the newspapers the whole process of Electronic Payments had arrived at an impasse.

That year the Dutch Postbank chaired the main consultative body of the combined major banks. We knew the chairman quite well because next to being a business partner he was also a close personal friend of our Sales and Marketing Director.

The chairman wanted to get Electronic Money Transfer off the ground. Not only for his company, the Dutch Postbank, was it vital that the costly giro cheques became a thing of the past but also on a personal level he wanted to score as the chairperson of this very important consultative body.

He came to visit the company regularly to talk about the latest developments and this year the Director-general had not only invited the Sales and Marketing Director but had asked me to join them as well. He had invited me to talk about our cooperation with the major Telecom operator regarding the 'Switch' of the credit card transactions.

I brought along a number of graphs and figures and explained what we had accomplished so far. He was genuinely interested and asked many detailed questions about the possibilities and in particular whether it was possible to 'Switch' direct debit transactions. Of course that was possible. I could tell from his body language that he was very enthusiastic about the whole operation and thanked me profusely. It was obvious that a lot was going on in his mind.

Two weeks later I received a phone call from his secretary inviting me to give a presentation about our 'Switch' for the complete consultative body of all the major banks. The chairman and vice-chairman of the major telecom operator were also invited. Now the 'games' would really begin and this meeting put an end to a period of silence.

I learned that innovation is good for a company and that through innovation a company can bring about a better market position.

In sales product development is of vital importance. Every salesperson needs to have something new to discuss on a regular basis. On the one hand to keep existing customers interested and on the other hand to attract new customers. Salespeople are not always pleased when new products are introduced. It takes the pattern out of their sales tactics. They have a sales pitch and that is pleasant to work with. Nevertheless, in order for a salesperson to stay ahead of the game it essential to introduce a new product or an adjustment. It keeps the product range up-to-date and the staff involved.

Selling at top level

The invitation to 'give a performance' for the major banks, including the important representatives of the major Telecom Operator made me feel nervous. I knew I had to peak during that meeting and that it was an excellent opportunity for my company to create a distinct profile. Also our partner, the major Telecom Operator could now present itself as a serious business partner for banks.

And of course I had to take into account the powerful position of the major banks we depended on. We had placed cash points at the Central Train Stations and were very successful partly because of the favourable guest user rates granted by the Postbank. I also knew that our partner, the major Telecom Operator was not regarded as yet as a 'trusted party'. I had to balance the different interest of all parties against the interests of my own company. The stakes were high.

What was I to say to them? What was it they wanted to hear? What was it they did not want to hear? Possible answers kept going round in my mind. I did not sleep too well in those days and I also experienced some personal problems since my wife kept demanding my attention during her nocturnal fighting sessions. I put together a concept presentation but somehow it did not feel right and I was so tired. One thing was absolutely clear I had to be on edge that particular day.

Once again I turned to my God for help. I asked him to bless my work and to help me. I spent some time in meditation and prayer until I finally fell asleep. Two nights later I woke up and I realised that all of a sudden I knew what I was going to say. I would tell them the history of my company and the implementation of Electronic Money Transfer to secure our company's future. So basically the real-life story of the events at my company. I felt liberated that night, thanked my God and slept well.

The night before the presentation I once again had to deal with problems concerning my wife. I went to bed late and on the day of the meeting I decided to cancel all meetings to rest a while and concentrate on what could possibly be the most important presentation in my life. I had never before been asked to give a presentation at such a high level and I had to do it on my own. There was nobody who could help me.

That afternoon I arrived at the office of the major bank on my own. The top bankers were already present in the conference room as were the directors of the major Telecom Operator. I received a warm welcome from the chairman and since I was acquainted with most people present I tried to hide my sense of tension by extending a hearty welcome to every one. I wanted to prevent a hostile atmosphere at all cost.

Next, the chairman invited me to give my presentation and I started off telling the story of my company, supported by appealing graphs and pictures relating to Electronic Money Transfer. I touched upon the fact that we had been of service to customers of all banks by offering cash withdrawals 24 hours a day for cheques and giro cheques when their regular bank branch office was closed. That subsequently the banks had decided to place cash points which led to a decreasing number of customers. As a result of that we had decided to place cash points as well (major investment) in order to win back our customers, for our cash points were conveniently located and we were able to be of service to customers of the combined banks once more.

That we knew that the major banks would set up a conjoined 'Switch' for debit card transactions but that my company and also our partner, the major Telecom Operator was increasingly confronted with credit card transactions, which is why we had decided to initiate a combined 'Switch' switch project for online authorisation and verification of credit card transactions. All this not with the intention of competing with the banks, but to secure my companies future!

During my presentation I felt supported by the chairman and the directors of the Telecom Operator because of their body language. I could tell that the other bankers were impressed by my story and previously had not been aware of the impact of Electronic Money Transfer on the prospects of my company. I saw respect in their eyes and once I finished my presentation I felt that I had done a good job. Together with the two directors of the Telecom Operator I left the conference room and they congratulated me on my solid performance and good presentation. They were pleased and our partnership was saved.

Back in my car I suddenly felt exhausted and lonely. I was drained of all energy. I did not want to go home because I was not able to deal with the situation back there. I parked my car in a lay-by along the motorway and thanked my God. I managed to relax a bit and slowly but surely I felt the energy returning and it felt good.

I learned that banks do not wish to harm to other companies with their actions. They want to offer financial services and products to all clients. My honest story had struck a chord.

At this point I wish to emphasise that eventually honesty is the best policy. Having said that, the truth can, of course, be expressed in different ways. When expressed in the correct wording the truth is the best option. Salespeople sometimes have a tendency towards adapting the message to the person they are dealing with. They wish to satisfy the prospect and/or customer in order to sell their products. Ultimately deliberate lies or holding back information will always backfire. It is therefore a short-term strategy.

Love cannot be bought

In those days I was having a hard time of it. My work was very absorbing but since I was successful it also generated energy. I could not enjoy my success though, because the problems with my wife were getting out of hand. So far we had been able to hide her outbursts from my daughter because she would not start her fits and discussions until after my daughter was asleep.

Things changed when my wife also started drinking during the day and went after my daughter as well. I tried to explain to my daughter the process my wife was going through. Her terrible youth, the death of her father, her relationship with her mother and the death of her favourite brother. I told her the whole story and asked her to be patient with her mother and try to help her mother get through this difficult period in her life.

Because of all the lengthy battles during the nights I could not possibly believe my wife still loved me. I decided to go and sleep in the spare room because I did not want to feel as if I was assaulting my wife whenever I wanted to engage in physical contact. Without love I would rather do without sex. I respected her and I did not want to take advantage of her.

I tried to make her life as agreeable to her as possible and gave her anything she wanted with regard to clothes, shoes and jewellery. She also wanted to get her driving licence and I paid for her lessons. She did need an awful lot of lessons and never passed the driving test. It cost me an absolute fortune and I even ended up in financial difficulties

At work I was called to account by the Bank Director; my own colleague would you believe. I was burning with shame and promised him to put my financial affairs in order. I did not refer to my domestic problems but decided to structure my personal finances to prevent similar incidents from happening.

One day I arrived home unexpectedly and found my wife and her driving instructor together in the kitchen. There was a certain intimate atmosphere and I almost felt like an intruder. It hurt me tremendously and I only managed to say 'hello' and went without saying another word to my study. I felt miserable and sad because I could no longer deny that this was the beginning of the end of my marriage for I did not want to spend my life with someone who did not love me.

Fortunately I derived satisfaction from soccer. I had given up on playing field soccer but they had roped me into becoming team coach. I had promised them I would, but not alone so I we had conjoined team coaches. Right before a match was to start I used to address some of the younger players individually.

This provoked quite a bit of comment from the other players because they all craved some personal attention and pep talk. That season we won the competition with an average team. A great experience that in the end took up more time than actually playing soccer. I decided to take up indoor soccer because it would be less of a strain on my ankles and it would take up less time.

I learned that it is impossible to buy love and solve the problems I was experiencing with money. Sports took my mind of things and also served to improve my managerial skills.

It's all sales

People are special creatures. No matter what we do, whether we try to help as many people as we can or whether we are self absorbed, ultimately we always serve our own best interest. For a salesperson this is an important fact to keep in mind. Never forget that the person you are talking to is always looking after 'number one'. This sounds incredible but even the most sociable person serves his own interests.

The sales of Pin Cash withdrawals

After the successful presentation of our conjoined 'Switch' computer for the bankers another heated discussion started in the Netherlands concerning the introduction of 'plastic currency' in retail.

The combined banks had their own organisation with their own 'Switch' computer and in addition to that there was our 'Switch' computer, which was regarded as the solution for the retailers. Banks only wanted to accept direct debit card transactions with a PIN code and we accepted credit card transactions. Both 'Switch' computers were suited for the acceptance of all 'plastic currency' retail transactions.

The discussion mainly focused on the transaction rates the banks intended to charge the retailers for each transaction. The largest Dutch retailer refused to pay the transaction rates since they thought the banks were overcharging. Because of that refusal the introduction of 'plastic currency' in the Netherlands had reached an impasse.

All the players in the 'plastic currency' market were aware of the fact that the major Telecom Operator and my company had embarked on a conjoined 'Switch' computer programme. In order to stir things up a bit our partner, the Telecom Operator, had introduced a standard rate per transaction that was significantly below the rate of the combined banks and was acceptable to the largest retailer in the Netherlands.

As was common knowledge, the combined banks and the major Telecom Operator were at that point in time discussing the options. As a result a secret working group had been established with the major banks and the Telecom Operator taking part. The objective was to examine whether the transaction rates could be reduced and the two 'Switch' organisations would be compared. I was asked to take part in the committee in a private capacity. My company was considered neutral and a neutral approach to the matter was what was required of me. It was a considerable honour and a reward for all the hard work I had put in.

It soon became clear that the combined banks were still divided. On the one hand there was the Dutch Postbank while on the other hand the other banks had joined forces. In addition to that, the management of the 'Switch' organisation also took part in the working group. All this, together with the major Telecom Operator formed four different 'camps' with their own interests to look after. The atmosphere was certainly not a friendly one and I was right in between the four camps as a neutral referee.

By means of comparing the two 'Switch' organisations the working group discovered that it was possible to reduce the transaction costs. This was good news for the retailers and my company. Now we only had to deal with the question which 'Switch' computer was to be used; ours or the one owned by the combined banks.

In those days my telephone would not stop ringing. They would ask me whether I was interested in taking up the position of Director of the 'Switch' organisation and what was to become of the current director? They were interested in my plans etc. etc. Both from the banking industry as well as the Telecom operator they were putting their feelers out. I was not interested in playing boss in a 'Switch' computer centre. I was dedicated to completing the automation plans for my company.

The discussion between the Telecom Operator and the banks took place at top level with the result that the combined banks remained responsible for the payment transactions, including the 'Switch' computer and the required organisation for the project. The Telecom Operator was not involved and I never managed to find out what the deal was. It was one of the best-kept secrets in the business.

The chairman of the combined banks committee (our business friend from the Postbank) lost no time in getting in touch with the largest retailer in The Netherlands to offer them a lower transaction rate and made a deal. It was the beginning of the successful introduction of electronic money transfer in the Netherlands.

I learned that every party involved in a business deal will look after its own interests. Fortunately I was capable of looking after the interests of my own company. My own interests were subordinate to that.

It's all sales

What we see is that each party plays its own part and has its own interests. Everyone looks after his own interests. You will make a difference if you are capable of looking after the interests of the other party while safeguarding those of your party at the same time. Take this into account when preparing a meeting.

Selling with a motivated department

The organisational set-up and development of my Automation Department was almost completed. The department consisted of about 30 staff in the sub divisions Development and Control, Administrative Organisation, Information Centre and the Calculus Centre. We installed different standard software packages for amongst others the Bank, Human Resources, the network and Finances.

Only the specific applications for the branch offices were still being developed. We had brought in consultants to deal with the tasks we did not have the expertise for and we had outsourced the programming for a 'fixed price and fixed date' to our regular supplier.

The introduction of standard software had left its mark on the departmental work processes. The Information Analysts were now much more occupied as Organisation Analyst and the Functional Comptrollers, who were very knowledgeable with regard to standard packages, could be of assistance to the end users by simply adapting the parameters in the standard software.

The result was that the Automation Department operated closely to the end users and was, therefore, more removed from the set up of the 'old' Automation Departments. As an additional result even I became more involved in the commercial running of the company.

Because of the total automation with all systems online and real-time every new product required lots of automation input. A move from Automation to Organisation and Commerce became apparent. I thought it was a great development and I was very proud of it. After all, the Automation Department is there to meet the requirements of the company's customers.

A dream was about to come true. And the only reason why this could happen was because of the young uninhibited staff that would not hold back because of knowledge attained at former employers and was capable of developing all their own material.

I still had to find a suitable Head of Development and Control. Two times in a row I had made a wrong choice. I was now doing the work myself but that took up a lot of time and energy and I wanted to contribute to the commercialisation of my company by means of Automation.

My company had employed one of our external consultants cum project leader for five years now. He was an amiable man and everyone got along with him quite well. The end-users were also pleased with him. He seemed suited for the position of Head of the Development and Control department so I decided to 'test the waters' and fortunately he was interested.

He was employed by one of our 'preferred suppliers', which made it difficult for us to take him on. I had to tread carefully on this one because in our contract we had included a clause stating that we would not try to take over staff employed by the other company. The Project Leader had made it clear that he would leave the company anyway, as soon as he was no longer assigned to my company. We decided to embark on the 'negotiating game' together. He was to inform his manager that he was interested in applying for the position of Head of Development and Control at my company. He would not tell him that I had already approached him.

His manager set up a meeting during which he informed me that he was not too pleased with recent developments. He totally overlooked the interests of the Project Leader but was only interested in the money involved. I decided to turn things around and my arguments focused on the interest of the Project Leader. If he were no longer allowed to work for my company he would resign anyway. The Manager came round to my point of view so we were able to make a deal satisfactory to both parties.

At the secretarial office of my department we had three secretaries: a Management Assistant, a Departmental Secretary and a part-time Support Secretary. A great team and they worked well together in a friendly atmosphere.

The three ladies were very different but complementary with regard to their behaviour. I had managed to keep my personal problems from them for quite a while but since I felt at ease with them, I could not help but talk to them occasionally about my daughter and myself. We were next to colleagues also friends. Things got more difficult when my wife started to make phone calls to the office while she was drunk. I had to inform my secretary about what was going on and I could no longer keep my private life, private. Fortunately she was very discrete about the whole matter and never said a word to anyone about it.

The (mostly young) employees in my department made me happy. It made me feel good to work for them and with them and I also noticed that together we were able to perform miracles. We were all very eager to win for our company. By means of the pleasant atmosphere and working relationships they also improved both on a personal and business level.

I learned once again that I enjoy working with young people; to coach them and see them improve. I was cut out for being a 'father figure' and it did not only motivate me but them as well.

It goes to show that it is important to use your own strong suits as a starting point because the natural ability to do things that suit you is important. This is different for every individual. But by just staying close to what you are good at, you can show your specialty, which can set you apart from others. Whereas one individual may possess a tremendous intellectual capacity, a different individual may be a very sociable person. Both are important in order to reach our goals.

A true 'Captain of Industry'

He was one of the most famous entrepreneurs in the Netherlands. He had built his Automation business from scratch and had turned it into a successful and respected enterprise. He was renowned and a popular speaker at seminars. He maintained close relationships with the government and all sectors of the business world. Almost every financial paper featured him and his successful company. He was what you call a true 'Captain of Industry'

My company was already doing business with this company because we had outsourced the technical maintenance of our technical infrastructure to them. And once a year a representative of the company would pay us a visit. It was more or less a courtesy call to assess whether we were still satisfied with the service they provided. This time the 'Captain of Industry' himself would come and pay us a visit.

The secretary to our Director-general phoned me to request my presence during this meeting. The Director-general was slightly nervous and asked me whether there were any problems he should know about with this supplier.

He just could not imagine that the 'Captain of Industry' could be interested in paying a personal visit to a mid size company like ours. As far as he was concerned there had to be problems. There were no problems; in fact we were quite pleased with this supplier.

The father of our current Director-general had been one of the founders of our company and his son had expanded the firm to a mid size company. It had always annoyed him that as far as the market was concerned our company was his father's enterprise. The aim of the Director-general was for the world to accept him on his own merits. This was not an easy thing to do and a familiar issue known as the problem of 'second generation entrepreneurs'.

The morning of the meeting the Director-general asked me to join him half an hour prior to the meeting so we could discuss the relationship we had with the supplier. I noticed that he was still nervous and suspicious with regard to the reason the 'Captain of Industry' had decided to come and visit us in person. I tried to convince him that it was only a courtesy call, nothing to worry about. I, for one, was not worried for I was quite looking forward to meet this interesting person.

The secretary showed him into the office. Facing us was a normal man in a trench coat. Not a macho, nothing authoritarian about him. He was one in thousand. As soon as the secretary had taken his coat, we had been introduced and coffee had been handed round, he took out a notepad and a pencil and put both items in front of him on the table. He started the conversation by thanking us for our time and then said "I would like to thank you for being my customer, for without customers my company couldn't exist". He then continued by saying "Please tell me whether there are any problems with our services" and picked up his pencil and notepad and started writing.

There were no problems and I noticed that the Director-general was starting to unwind and feel at ease. It turned out to be a pleasant and constructive meeting and we spent some time discussing the latest market developments.

I learned that I appreciated dealing with successful people. Especially people who were successful but who at the same time had not lost their human touch and had kept their feet firmly on the ground. I respected people who could do this and I definitely wanted to learn how to achieve this.

It's all sales

As Jim Collins put it in his book "From Goods to Great"; successful and inspired people are more successful in the long run if they remain true to themselves. They make a difference not because of what they know, but because of what they are! Not only knowledge and skills will make you a perfect manager, salesperson, physician or teacher. No, the determining factor is YOU! Think 'big' and have a 'small' attitude. Humanity + Power = Success.

Soccer as a sales instrument

Our partner, the major Telecom Operator, was very grateful to me because of our successful co-operation, but they were especially grateful for the fact that their company was now considered an equal partner in the market and could play an important part in the 'Electronic Payment' market in the Netherlands.

They knew I was a great soccer fan and they were main sponsor of the Dutch national soccer team. I was invited to watch a number of matches of our national team for the European and World Championships. To me this represented a wonderful way to relax, for I could thoroughly enjoy watching a good match.

My first invitation was to a qualifying match abroad. On our way to the match I was seated on the plane right in between the Chairman and the Vice-Chairman of the major Telecom Operator. All the others present were looking at me and probably wondering who I was and what I had done to deserve this special treatment. I, however, only talked about soccer and it was clear that my attitude was appreciated. It was time for some serious soccer.

At the next invitation I ended up sitting on the coach next to the Chairman and his son. He had invited me especially because he wanted to discuss soccer and nothing but soccer. He told me that he got often invited to a Skybox to watch a match. He did not like that much though, because in his eyes it had nothing to do with soccer. To cheer for a goal was 'not done'. He enjoyed it much more to be out on the stand, casually dressed and watch the match from there. I could not agree with him more and we only discussed soccer. His son beamed with delight. I respected him tremendously because he really did have a brilliant business mind while at the same time keeping his feet firmly on the ground. Later on in life he became even more successful. I was proud to have known him.

At the invitation of the vice-chairman I visited a match for the World Championship on another continent. In order to get everyone there The Telecom Operator had chartered the plane from the MGM Film Company. Usually the plane could seat 250 people but for the special occasion it was fitted out with a real bar and a seating capacity for 50 people. All very decadent. Once again I was seated at the front of the plane, close to the bar and all of a sudden I realised I was sitting on a chair that had once been used by Madonna. Also the hotel rooms were splendid and I was lodged in an apartment with all the trimmings.

I was not feeling well in those days, though. The many personal problems I was facing were wearing me out. I felt lonely and alone and I was not too keen on talking to anyone. I tried to use this trip to come to terms with the issues I had to deal with.

I noticed that quite a few Telecom Managers surrounded the Vice-Chairman, who was accompanied by his wife. They were all trying to get in his good books. The wife of the Vice-Chairman smoked cigars so all the other women all of a sudden had this urge to smoke cigars as well. Unfortunately for most of them it was their first time and there was no end to their coughing and gasping. Apparently they thought their husbands' career prospects were worth this. It made me laugh, but I could not help but notice that the vice-chairman was surrounded too much by his own vassals and that he enjoyed that perhaps a bit too much.

Once we were on our way to the stadium he came to walk next to me all of a sudden and asked me whether I was having a good time. I thanked him for inviting me but also added that I was only there for the soccer match.

I learned that the Chairman and Vice-Chairman were very important to the Telecom Operator as a team. This can only work out if you remain with your feet firmly on the ground and if you can determine who your real friends are and who are not.

It's all sales

Whenever you display behaviour that everyone expects from you, you will not be able to stand out from the rest. Sales is of course all about setting yourself apart from the rest. Particularly in situations like these when you take somebody away from his natural surroundings to please him. How can you stand out if you meet each other in different surroundings and different circumstances? You will surely be noticed if you tell a bit more about yourself and encourage others to show a bit of the private side of their lives.

Selling like a 'rocket'

This man was very important for the sales process of my automation plans in our company. The firm had employed him for many years, but now he was responsible for the installation of all hardware at the offices of all staff in my department. He knew everyone in all of our 80 offices and they all knew him. They had nicknamed him 'the rocket' because with his lease car he used to drive at an incredible speed throughout the whole country.

He loved our company and at the same time his approach towards service and his positive attitude were respected. He did not only install the hardware, he also never considered it beneath him to repair the coffee machine as well. All in a day's work. Whenever he came to the head office I always made sure we had the chance to talk while enjoying a cup of coffee.

He would then inform me about the problems 'in the field' and from him I learned what the real issues were at the offices and I could take action to prevent a situation from escalating. I also disclosed my automation plans to him so he in turn could put staff at the offices at ease. To me he was an important source of information the so-called voice of the customers.

Yet he was also an emotional person and his lease car meant the world to him. After all he practically lived in his car. Sometimes I had to help him circumvent some minor rules regarding his lease car and whenever bonuses were to be allocated I made sure he received what was due to him. He deserved every penny because his commitment and dedication were unsurpassed.

When his 25th anniversary was due, he invited everyone in the department. Together with my secretaries and the colleagues we put together a great song for him as a token of our appreciation.

Once we arrived at the venue we had not yet rehearsed the song. As soon as everyone had arrived I asked all those involved to step outside to rehearse the song. As it happened the venue was located right in the centre of a village and our rehearsal coincided with the late opening hours of the shops. We rehearsed our song in the village square, which convinced some of the locals that we represented the Salvation Army and they wanted to donate cash, much to the amusement of us all.

Back in the function room we delivered our song like true larks. Our 'rocket' thoroughly enjoyed our performance and tears of emotion were running down his cheeks. And that was how it should be. Our 'rocket' was a true family man and he adored his wife and children. His daughter was therefore also present and had brought her boyfriend along. But as soon as I saw them together I noticed that something was amiss. I did not pay any attention to it at the time.

One year later during an office party in a restaurant the 'rocket' was also present. I could not help but notice that he did not look happy. He was not cheerful and seemed depressed. I ordered two beers from the bar, walked up to him and asked him how he was doing. He then told me that his daughter and son-in-law had split up. He was upset with his daughter because he thought the world of his son-in-law. As a result the daughter no longer visited her parents but the ex son-in-law still came by the house quite often. He started to cry because both him and his wife missed their daughter so much.

My God put the right words into my mouth. I told the 'rocket' that whatever happened he always had to take sides with his daughter and not his son-in-law. No matter what, she would always be his daughter and it was better for family relationships that he would respect his daughter's choices. It was after all her life and for a parent it felt more natural to side with your daughter. As her father he had to support her through thick and thin. My words obviously struck a cord because he looked relieved. He went to the bar to get me beer and went on to enjoy the rest of the party.

One week later the 'rocket' called me and told me that he and his wife had contacted their daughter and that she would pay them a visit the next day. He sounded relieved and happy and thanked me profusely. The whole affair made me feel 'grateful and happy'.

Again I learned that children are important to us. You cannot always rely on your brain but that you have to listen to your heart. To support them no matter what happens, that is what it is all about. I thanked my God for showing me the wisdom of it all.

In one of the final paragraphs it says "the whole affair made me feel grateful and happy." This is an expression that is valid especially for salespeople. Salespeople are often trained in conversation techniques and are therefore capable of offering advice to their customers. This is what sets one salesperson apart from the other. If a piece of advice turns out to be successful you could brag about it and take advantage of it. The real trick is to be modest about the whole affair but make sure he does not forget what you have done for him. As a result of this the customer will want to make it up to you, a sentiment from which you will benefit. Laying it on with a trowel will only backfire. `Be modest when it comes to big things and be noble when it comes to small matters´.

Microsoft Windows and the market

It was truly a major development when Microsoft launched Windows. It was the product everyone had been waiting for since most people were dissatisfied with what IBM had to offer.

At my company we used PCs as a production computer in our offices and they were linked up to each other through a local network. For these production PCs we were not about to use Windows for we did not consider Windows to be reliable enough. We did use Windows for our stand alone PCs, though. Everybody was eager to have Windows installed despite its unreliability and the fact that the only way to solve problems was to re-start the PC.

The way in which Microsoft had introduced the product Windows to the market presented a unique and novel marketing approach to the world. As far as the marketing professionals were concerned the whole world had been turned upside down. Whole seminars were dedicated to the product launch of Windows. First have the product installed for free and as soon as the users are acquainted with the product, present them with the bill. A truly unique concept that because of its success commanded respect and was often copied.

Later on I talked to a senior Sales Director at IBM and he had to acknowledge that the success of Windows was the greatest opportunity they had missed out on in the history of IBM.

The rise of the PC and Windows was of extreme importance to me since it enabled me to realise my Information and Automation Plan. A major break-through for everyone involved in automation.

What I learned was that it is relatively simple to sell a product and sell it successfully at that if everyone has awaited it. Yet the first step always remains to find investors who are also willing to believe in the product.

The million-dollar question remains; how do you develop a product the whole world is waiting for? One step in the right direction is careful market analysis. If you take into consideration that only 20% of the products that are introduced to the market actually are successful, it will be clear that also a fair amount of luck is involved. However, a product that is easy to sell will make salespeople obsolete. If that is the case the product can be sold through other channels. Fortunately many products do need the added value of personal sales.

Abusing a gentlemen's agreement

The Director-general of our company strongly believed in the positive effects of good relationships between our company and other companies. It was also very important for the firm regarding the neutral position we wanted to maintain in the world of finance that we maintained good relationships with other financial institutions. And not only as far as the aforementioned companies are concerned also for shareholders, the works council, our suppliers and so on, he believed good relationships to be essential. The Director-general had turned maintaining a friendly and relaxed atmosphere during business lunches and dinners into a fine art.

I, for one, was all business. On most occasions I was too passionate about business to actually enjoy a business lunch or dinner. I did manage to learn quite a few things from the Director-general, though. The main difference was that I kept business and private separately. Not every business associate was a real friend as far as I was concerned.

The Interim Automation Manager, the person who had introduced me to the company, ran a small software company. This company had acquired the position of 'preferred supplier' with our company. The same company also employed the son of the Director-general, who wanted to embark on a career in automation after graduation. This is what we referred to as a gentlemen's agreement, something that was not mentioned.

The Director had told me though, and I did not think it could do any harm, as long as I was not supposed to keep the company as a 'preferred supplier' if they were not meeting our requirements. Even though I never said anything, the word about the Director-general's son's employment spread quickly. They often asked me for my opinion on the matter. It was grist to the mill of those opposing the Director-general.

In the meantime the small software company had been taken over by a larger software company; a change that would benefit me because it left me with more options. The new software company now became preferred supplier'. The Director of the new software company was what we called a genuine 'IT cowboy'. He had started his company from scratch and had turned it into a successful business. He did not fit in with the bankers. He was of course aware of the 'gentlemen's agreement' concerning the employment of our Director-general's son. At some point we both had been invited to lunch by the ' IT cowboy'. I noticed that the Director-general did not like the 'IT cowboy' much and he conveyed his hopes that the cowboy would not say a word about his son. He was prepared, though.

We arrived at the restaurant before our host and the first thing he said upon arrival was that the Director-general's son was doing a great job for the company. I could tell from the look on his face that the Director-general did not appreciate this at all but he just nodded and changed the subject.

I learned that you always have to respect a 'gentlemen's agreement' irrespective of any other business you might be involved in.

It's all sales

A salesperson can get confronted with information he picked up from customers. It might be tempting to help out another customer with this information. The strength of a salesperson lies in the fact whether he can refrain from using this information. If you do use this sensitive information it will always backfire which can lead to the loss of a customer and also the loss of self-esteem. It goes without saying that a salesperson will use all the information available to him to determine his own strategy and to carry it out.

Not going to sell 'bugs'

The meetings of the user group of our Standard Banking System changed in perspective ever since the supplier decided to sponsor them. The supplier would usually organise events at a spectacular hotel on a beautiful location somewhere in Europe.

The user group would meet prior to the meeting without the supplier for about an hour or so to discuss possible problems with the supplier. Towards the end of the event the supplier would be asked to answer questions. The charismatic chairperson always embarked on these question-and-answer sessions with lots of flair.

The supplier used these events as a sales instrument and also asked prospective customers to take part in order to get to know other users. Quite often a contract would be signed during these events.

As co-founder of the user group I knew most of those present. Well, most of them knew me since most had visited my company for reference purposes. I enjoyed attending those meetings and liked catching up on the latest developments with my business friends. In addition to that, it was always pleasant to experience that the supplier practically worshipped me and the chairman never stopped calling me his best salesperson.

By that time a number of Dutch users had joined the user group and during these events we teamed up and discussed the software related problems. The main topic of these meetings was the standard software and the supplier. Many suppliers enjoyed it tremendously to talk incessantly about their 'bugs'. The team of Dutch users on the other hand also wanted to have a bit of fun and relax. Usually during the second night of the event a dinner-dance would be organised by the supplier. It was common practice that the Dutch group of users ended up at the same table to which we would only invite users who were not eager to discuss their 'bugs'. We had a lot of fun during these evenings and our table had already earned a reputation with the other users and the supplier. We made the most of these events and had a wonderful time.

Usually a famous guest speaker was invited to address the group and it was not always easy to please all those present. On one occasion they had invited the former foreign secretary of the US to deliver a speech on the Cold War. His talk did not go down well with the delegates from the Eastern European Countries, who left the room in protest.

On another occasion a Can-Can dance group from Paris had been invited. This time the delegates from the Arab countries left the room in protest. Fortunately on most occasions there were no incidents and the highlight was usually the final speech by the charismatic Chairperson. More often than not he would put me in the limelight and called me his best salesperson. I did not particularly cherish this turn of phrase because I did not want to be called a salesperson for I did not want to be a salesperson.

Apart from the fun and games these events also served to discuss the latest financial developments in the world and devise new modules together with he supplier. My company took an active part in these developments and together with other members of the user group compiled the specifications for the EURO module. The supplier showed his gratitude by offering to sell the module to us at half price. Once again the user group had proven its worth.

I learned that co-operating with other parties is difficult unless there is something to be gained for all those involved. User groups can have an added value for all those taking part.

It's all sales

Tip: Major customers usually have access to extensive facilities a salesperson can make use of. For example by organising a sales meeting at the customer's company. The customer often considers it an honour to provide the means.

Selling a reorganisation

My Information and Automation Plan for the company had by now been put into effect almost completely. The standard systems in the back office were operational 24 hours a day and the same could apply to the network to and from offices and the front office systems at the offices. My department had been set up with professional staff who were familiar with the company's processes and had gained extensive knowledge regarding the (standard) systems.

By means of using standard software of which the parameters could be adjusted if necessary, a shift had become apparent from automation knowledge towards organisation and process knowledge. We were operating with a close link to the end users.

By now, as far as I was concerned, the fun had worn off. I knew I was keen on implementing changes but not so much on controlling the process. I started to feel this itch again and I found myself looking for new challenges. I felt that the Director-general would respect whatever I chose to do and he was aware of the fact that I was looking for something new to sink my teeth into. On the other hand he also did not want to lose me.

Within the company things kept changing as well. My friend the old Bank Director had been replaced. Also a new Director had been appointed who was the intended successor of the Director-General. In addition a new Marketing Director had been appointed but on the whole the old hands were still on deck.

Especially the Financial Comptroller was still firmly in charge and made life difficult for the new comers to the company. The company had to change and new products had to be introduced in order to secure the company's future, yet this proved to be difficult because changes met with opposition. We did manage to introduce some new products and established offices in other countries. We intended to explore the boundaries of the EURO zone.

All these changes in management led to an inevitable reorganisation and when the Director-general discussed the matter with me I asked him whether the General and Technical Support Services Department could be assigned to me as well. I had already noticed that a combination of automation and general and technical support services would lead to increased efficiency and effectiveness.

The Director-general agreed to this and in addition appointed me a permanent member of the Board of Directors and I was also assigned the highest level of procuration. The Steering Committee was also part of the Board of Director's meeting. The General and Technical Support Services Department comprised purchasing, mail room, catering, security, company driver and storage.

When it came to the firm's procuration authorisation; I only used it when I knew what I was actually signing. I refused to put my name to documents of which I did not know what they contained. Yes, I had definitely learned my lesson with previous employers.

In those days many seminars had been organised regarding purchasing and how to optimise procedures. I attended some of these seminars and outside office hours I spent quite some time on studying the ins and outs of these new departments. I intended to compile an integration and optimisation plan.

The Head of General and Technical Support Services was the former Head of the Automation department and also Chairman of the Works Council. He was also known as The King of Corridor Chat. I did not find it difficult to manage him.

This meant though that I had to use two different styles of management. For the highly developed Automation team I was the manager-coach whereas to those employed in the General and Technical Support Department I had to be manger-decision maker. They were pleased as long as they thought their input about the way the apartment was run was appreciated and they were pleased to have someone who listened to them. To me the combination presented a new challenge.

I learned that by now I was well aware of my own strengths and weaknesses. I knew I liked challenges and approached everything as a project that had to be completed. Fortunately I was also capable to adapt my style of management to what the situation demanded.

It's all sales

Self-awareness is essential. You see this happen in many companies; the excellent salesperson who is promoted to a managerial position. The company directors hope that in promoting him he will be able to teach the other salespeople the tricks of the trade. It is only a matter of time before the newly promoted salesperson is in a fix. Selling through other people is a completely different job altogether.

The new Account Manager

This supplier was carefully selected. The company was global market leader and our shareholders were also among their customers. In my automation plans the hardware had been selected on the basis of the standard software. Fortunately the standard software was devised for it to be compatible with the hardware of the market leader. As a mid size enterprise you cannot afford to re-invent the wheel. Everything had to be standardised.

Its leading market position had made this supplier arrogant. They had adopted an attitude as if they were to determine whether a customer was to invest in hardware or not. Their products were beyond the need of salespeople.

In accordance with company policy they appointed a new Account Manager every year. The company was expanding at such a speed that internal promotion also accelerated. I enjoyed playing games with the arrogant salespeople. Over the past few years I had presented my Automation Plan on many occasions to several managers and salespeople within the different layers of their organisation. I could therefore assume that the people at the supplying company had some idea of what my company was doing and what we had planned.

That is not the way things worked for our supplier. The new Account Manager would always come and visit without his predecessor and asked me after our plans. I pretended to be surprised that he was not informed and sent him back to his head office to check with his predecessor. Once that had been accomplished he could return.

On some occasions the Account Manager was completely taken aback and asked me timidly whether he was allowed to finish his cup of coffee before he left. Usually the Account Managers would make a new appointment and would be better prepared. I admit I was not exactly nice to them but I did buy their computers.

On one occasion another Account Manager presented himself and I played my little game with him as well. Unfortunately this one flew off the handle and pointed out to me that I was not in his top ten of preferred clients. As far as he was concerned I was only small fry. I sent him packing straight away and this guy was certainly not allowed to finish his cup of coffee. The same afternoon I got in touch with his manager and I was assigned a new Account Manager, one who had done his 'homework'.

I learned that major suppliers can become arrogant because of their successful products. They know that you need them and they try to take advantage of that. Sometimes they forget, though, that customer is always King.

It is as in a marriage. As soon as dependence enters, one of those involved starts to be more domineering. This happens consciously but sometimes also subconsciously. If you know that your customer needs you, your approach will differ. The true art of selling is not to take advantage of this situation but to convince the customer with the right arguments that meet the customer's requirements (What he thinks is important).

Losing out on a deal every step of the way

It was no longer feasible to keep my domestic problems hidden. My wife called the office while she was drunk and the only thing I could do was go home, clean the house and wait for my daughter to come home. It was not easy because my wife was always angry with me and wanted to pick a fight. Still, no matter what, my daughter was always top priority.

One day I arrived home unexpectedly and I caught my wife sitting on our doctor's lap and she was kissing him. It hurt me tremendously and I went straight to my study. Inside I was burning with rage and I finally understood why the doctor had been opposed to my wife seeking professional help for her problems.

Over a period of time she had paid quite a number of visits to our doctor and he of course did not want this to be known. If this affair were to become public knowledge he would be struck off the register. I decided to keep the matter to myself mainly because I did not want to harm my wife's reputation. It dawned upon me that I had no feelings left for my wife. Our marriage was over.

During one of her outbursts of anger we were in the kitchen together with our dog Bobo. Bobo was sleeping in its dog basket. All of a sudden it turned very cold in the kitchen. Not just a matter of the temperature dropping but it felt like the cold of death. My wife fell into a trance and started talking to her father who had been dead for quite some time and who was supposed to be sitting opposite me. She was swearing at her father and told him to stay away from Bobo. Bobo jumped up from its basket as if stung and wanted to go outside immediately. I opened the kitchen door and Bobo and I went outside. After a while, we were warmed up sufficiently and I wanted to return to the house. Bobo resisted and fought tooth and nail to stay outside. When I had finally managed to get the dog inside the house my wife had already departed to her bedroom.

Bobo suffered from the atmosphere in our house. The fights and the lack of love and attention got to him, our beautiful blond Bouvier des Flandres. He was a very unhappy dog and one day when I got back from work I found him in de garden. It was obvious that Bobo was ill. I took him to the vet straight away and as it turned out our dog suffered from lung cancer. It would be best to have Bobo humanely euthanized.

I was devastated because Bobo had been a dear friend and had always been around. Also, Bobo had been my daughter's best friend for they had grown up together. When I got home and told my family the outcome of my trip to the vet my daughter was very sad. That same night my wife removed every single item that reminded her of Bobo. I never understood why she had to do that immediately.

In spite of the miserable time I had of it, I kept my promise not to divorce my wife until she had found a way of dealing with her problems. I did not want to leave her alone. Moreover, I wanted to wait for the sake of my daughter. She was doing reasonably well in school and I did not want to upset her life. It became increasingly difficult to put up with it though, because all the love I had felt for my wife had vanished. We slept in separate rooms and avoided each other whenever we possibly could. Slowly but surely my wife had lost all credit with me.

Not too many people around us knew about our problems. Only our next-door neighbours and my secretary were aware of our differences but both our families were kept in the dark.

I learned that it was not easy for me, a winner, to accept that I was fighting a losing battle. There were forces in play I could not overcome. Without love you cannot win a battle like this one. But please, let de dead rest in peace.

It's all sales

Not being awarded an assignment is a 'silent fear' of every salesperson since most of the time you have invested some time and effort into getting the order. This is often a reason why salespeople tend to postpone the moment of asking for an order. Instead of asking the customer for an order they will introduce more arguments; arguments which are often not relevant for the customer. Getting 'NO' for an answer inspires fear in many salespeople. However, getting no for an answer offers new possibilities to find out why the customer will not place an order. He will, whether he is aware of this or not, inform you on why he is not going to award you an order. Through this you will find out how his mind works. Mostly some of the counter arguments are based on misunderstandings, something that is not quite clear or an assumption. At that stage you are finally able to respond. So in fact you should be glad with getting 'No' for an answer.

The computer centre is not for sale

The computer centre was part of my Automation Department and I intended to integrate the computer centre with the General and Technical Support Service Department in order to increase efficiency and effectiveness. The computer centre was responsible for the operational control of the important Back office systems of our company. The security surrounding the entire operation was at the level demanded by the Dutch National Bank.

One of our preferred suppliers had in the past been responsible for the production of our Banking System. In order to compensate for the loss of revenue we had assigned a number of their consultants to the implementation of the Standard Banking System. Now that the job was completed the company was losing out on a regular source of income.

Our Director-general had been on friendly terms with the Director of the preferred supplier and they met for lunch on a regular basis. The usual outcome of these lunch meetings was that I had to put in an appearance and explain the ins and outs of my automation plans. This time the Director had convinced our Director-general that it would be in his best interest to allow research to be carried out to determine whether his company should take over our calculus centre. Allegedly they could do the same job at a better price.

The supplier, in the mean time, appointed a number of consultants who were to carry out the research. I was left no other choice but to co-operate while I was convinced that it would be a waste of time and money because it was almost impossible to run the different programs more efficiently and effectively.

I had included in my automation policy that we would always be on the lookout for co-operation in order to reduce costs. Because of this I did not have a leg to stand on to stop this research. I did not appreciate this latest decision of the Director-general. I would have preferred it if he had discussed the issue with me first. I felt as if I had painted myself into a corner and it did not feel right. I was watchful and I knew they had to come up with a good plan in order to convince me.

The consultants who were to carry out their research needed quite a lot of financial background info and in order to provide the required info I had set up a meeting with our Financial Comptroller. The Comptroller and I did not see eye to eye and in the past we had been at loggerheads on my many occasions. As soon as he discovered what kind of information the consultants needed he was livid. He strongly opposed the outsourcing of our calculus centre since he was a satisfied end user. He was not aware that by saying this he actually paid me a compliment. I said nothing though, and bided my time. I adopted a neutral approach but inside I could not help but laugh.

As soon as the consultants had compiled their proposal all the members of the Board of Directors of both companies had been invited to this top-notch dinner to introduce the findings of their research. I was apprehensive and I was not sure whether the beautiful surroundings in which the findings were presented would be to our advantage. I had much rather had the opportunity to study the report beforehand.

Their presentation was not a good one and the Comptroller and I were not convinced. Inside I was ill at ease and I had no idea of what was on my plate. Fortunately I was able to hide my feelings but this did take up a lot of energy. It was decided to put the report on the agenda of the next board meeting and to reach a decision on whether or not to outsource the calculus centre.

I was in two minds about what to do next. Their proposal was not up to scratch but I knew that whatever objections I would raise I would not be taken seriously because I had something to lose. I talked through the proposal with our external Auditor and he also opposed the proposition because as far as he was concerned the Dutch National Bank had not yet approved the outsourcing of banking systems. This was a solid argument but I had to broach the subject in guarded terms and play the game carefully.

I took the utmost care when writing down my response. I tried to come across as neutral and suggested that we consulted legislation concerning outsourcing issued by the Dutch National bank before deciding on the matter.

During the board meeting the Financial Comptroller lost no time in arguing that he was opposed to the proposal and help also came from unexpected quarters. The new Bank Director, who happened to be quite satisfied with the services provided by the calculus centre, also opposed the proposal. As it turned out the decision was made without too many problems and the Director-general used the argument of the rules issued by the Dutch National Bank as the reason why our company could not go ahead with the plans.

I learned to control my emotions when it came to doing business. It was never easy though and it took up a lot of energy. Most cases are decided on the basis of good arguments and not on an emotional basis.

It is funny but emotion in business is not such a bad idea after all. It is, however, not to be recommended to use emotions to the extreme. It is essential that a salesperson is regarded as being authentic. This goes with personal emotional feelings. His smile, the earnest look on his face, his surprise, and his reservations. What always remains is that a salesperson can remain spontaneous although you have to make sure that you play it smart.

Selling the love for a soccer team

This youngster was the son of an acquaintance. His mother and her (somewhat younger) boyfriend ran a tanning studio. That is where I had met them. He was attending the School for Business Administration and Finance and he had asked me whether he could take an internship at my department. I decided I wanted to help him and I hoped I could take him on as a full time employee as soon as he had graduated.

He was young and dynamic but still had a lot to learn. He was a student and this was his first experience with a regular day job and it was not easy for him work eight hours a day and stick to the rules laid down by an employer. He had to get used to having colleagues being sociable, schedule appointments and show up on time etc. etc. But on the whole I thought he was a pleasant character and my secretary thought so too. We were to become his business father and mother.

In his spare time he was an avid soccer player and played in his village's first team. In addition to that he was a huge fan of the famous soccer club Inter Milan. His mother's boyfriend had managed to secure two tickets for the Derby Inter Milan versus AC Milan and had made travel arrangement to attend the match. He told my secretary all about this great trip he had lined up. They were to leave on a Thursday and return on a Monday evening. He had forgotten, though, to inform me and ask permission since I was his manager.

I decided to teach him a valuable lesson. I had informed my secretary of my intentions and she was happy to play along. I invited him into my office to discuss his planning schedule. We compiled a rather tight schedule and towards the end of the meeting I could do nothing but conclude that given the tight schedule he would not be able to take any leave.

He left the meeting and told my secretary about the outcome. She then asked whether he had asked permission to take a couple of days off to attend the soccer match. He told her he had not. "Well, in that case you have a big problem on your hands" was her response adding that he should have asked my permission before he made the arrangements. He became very nervous and did not know what to do.

That same night I phoned his mother, since he was out on the soccer pitch I knew I could do so without him knowing about it. I told her about my little plan and asked her whether she wanted to co-operate. She laughed and said that now she understood why he had returned home in such a foul mood. She appreciated my approach of her 'macho' son. I told her to advise her son to make an appointment with me and so he did. My secretary had not been very accommodating when he approached her to set up a meeting but it was a matter of great importance to him to talk to me before that Thursday.

The day before he was to leave I had a serious conversation with him. I came into my office accompanied by my secretary. And believe me; I have never heard so many emotional, rational and irrational arguments from somebody who wanted to convince me of something. I was enjoying all this and he promised to work overtime every single night and to work weekends to meet his deadlines. Eventually I did give him permission to take a few days off. He was a true fan of Inter Milan and at the same time he learned that he had to stick to the rules.

I learned that I enjoyed coaching young people and to help them improve not only their skills but also their approach and attitude. According to his mother this youngster had named me his personal guru.

It's all sales

Irrespective of this story it is always important to be aware of the fact that you need others to reach your goals. In this case the secretary and the mother. It is therefore clear that it is easy to get a result. In the same way you can involve others in the selling and decision making process. Try to get a good idea who would be suitable in helping in each particular case. Have you already considered existing satisfied customers?

Selling a two party strategy

Even though we were a mid sized company we had been able to play an important part in the introduction of Electronic Payment in the Netherlands. As a result we had positioned cash points in our offices of all banks. Moreover, we had accomplished that our service desks would accept Pin Payments through all banks including the Dutch Postbank for our services and goods. We were on friendly terms with both the Postbank as well as the other banks.

Unfortunately there were still two separate systems to operate the cash points. On the one hand we had the cash points serving only the Postbank customers and on the other hand the cash points serving customers of all other banks by means of the guest user principle.

We had installed blocs of duo cash points and this system proved very profitable to us. At first the system had seemed a threat to our revenue but we had been able to turn it into a source of profit.

In one of our offices close to the border we had installed an exchange point for trial purposes. The customer would have to feed bank notes into the machine and determine in which currency he would like to have his money exchanged.

The exchange point was not a big success. As it turned out people do not like putting bank notes in a machine if they are not sure other bank notes will eventually appear. We probably all share experiences with cigarette machines you would put your money in and did not deliver the goods.

The exchange point had been quite an investment and we had to come up with a solution to generate return on investment. I came up with the idea to position a cash machine in the exchange point. Now the customer no longer had to insert bank notes but could withdraw foreign currencies with his bankcard or debit card. We discussed the solution with the supplier of the exchange point and he liked the idea. We decided to split the costs for adapting the machine.

We placed the new exchange point in a wall of one of our offices and indeed it worked. I realised that if we were to replace the foreign currencies with Dutch bank notes we would have created the first cash point that would accept cards issued by both the Postbank and the other combined banks. Because of the friendly co-operation we had with the Postbank we decided not to act upon this knowledge. We did inform our partners and they accepted and respected our decision.

Not long after we had placed our exchange point, one of the major banks also placed one at our national airport. Our innovation had not gone by unnoticed.

I learned that you have to respect your business friends. A gentlemen's agreement.

When it is to your best interest to remain on friendly terms with a customer, this requires a certain kind of behaviour. As a rule you always treat your customers with respect. Yet a salesperson does not have to be a friend to all and does not have to hide his personality. A true salesperson always keeps his own interests at heart and is involved in networking also in his spare time. In the end good relationships generate trade.

Losing my best friend

My best friend was a unique human being. I had met him when we both played in the same soccer team and I had been married for about two years. He wore his hair long, wore several layers of sweaters and always wore clogs. He also was in the habit of using the same diary for several years in a row because he thought it was a waste to throw it out after only one year. That is why he hardly ever showed up on the assigned date. He was a student of econometrics at the University in the city he lived in.

We immediately hit it off and became good friends. We were also both members of the editorial committee of the soccer club newsletter and had quite a few enjoyable evenings together. He was a regular visitor to our house and also became firm friends with my wife. He was also in the habit of visiting our home when I was not around, to talk to my wife.

He was a bit of an eccentric and lived in a small house. In order to save energy he had fixed plastic sheets in front of his windows. It was always freezing in his house but that did not bother him for he would simply wear an extra sweater. His neighbour kept two rats as pets. It was quite something else when the two rats sat on her shoulders.

We were invited when he took his doctorate degree and yes he did wear the mandatory dinner jacket to the ceremony yet he had also managed to dye his clogs black. At the time they accepted his behaviour because he was considered a genius. He was appointed professor at a University.

Sometimes I would visit him unannounced and most of the times I did he was not alone. There were always beautiful female students at his place. He treated them badly and without respect. He did tell me though that he was unhappy and would like to have a wife and partner to love and be loved. I tried to tell him in diplomatic terms that it would help if he were to change his lifestyle and behaviour. His surroundings were not of the kind a woman would be comfortable in and the way he treated women certainly was not the way to attract their attention. He always listened attentively to whatever I had to say on the matter and I did feel I got the message across.

One day he paid me an unexpected visit at the office. I did not know what hit me and I immediately took some time off to talk to him. He wanted to discuss a problem with me. The board of the University had told him that his behaviour had become unacceptable and that he was to dress appropriately in the future. He did not understand why all of a sudden he had to change, but I could tell from the look in his eyes that something was wrong.

I asked him outright whether he was using drugs. He nodded in agreement and I urged him angrily to stop. I also told him that eccentric behaviour was only considered acceptable if it was matched by extraordinary accomplishments. He had probably neglected his work, was therefore no longer special and was asked to behave normally.

He took my advice in his stride, changed his lifestyle and stopped taking drugs. Later on he was appointed professor at another University. I used to stop by his house unannounced to see whether he was still 'clean'.

I had also talked to him about the problems between my wife and me and I had also told him that I would wait with taking far-reaching decisions until she had come to terms with her problems. One day my wife went to visit him on her own for the day. She had asked me to come and pick her up. When I arrived at my friend's house that night I could not help but notice there was something going on between them and I noticed them exchanging meaningful glances. My wife did not want to go home with me. I felt ill at ease and it hurt me. I never said anything, but it became crystal clear what my future was going to be like.

One month later my friend came to visit us. My wife sat next to him, playing with his hair. It was torture for me to watch them, especially because I could feel there was something-special going on between them. I was not sure whether their relationship was purely platonic. By watching them together I felt once more that my marriage was over.

I could for the life of me not understand my friend's behaviour. As far as I was concerned best friends respected each other and stayed clear of each other's wives. My best friend, however, did not play by those rules. If I could not trust my wife and my best friend, who could I trust? Was I really that stupid and naïve?

I learned that all these incidents with my wife served to help me make up my mind about our marriage. It was about time to take some major decisions concerning my life. But I was feeling lonelier than ever for I did not know whom to trust anymore.

Also in sales trust is a tricky subject. When you have a good relationship with your customer you might believe every word he says and most of the time rightly so. But you will always be skating on thin ice. It is better to keep an open mind (on balance everyone is looking after his own interests). As soon as you are capable of asking relevant check questions, you will value someone properly.

Establishing a global user group

In order to 'Switch' electronic payment transactions we made use of a standard software package, in co-operation with a major Dutch Telecom Operator. The standard package was used globally and the supplier also used retailers in several countries to sell his products. Together with the Dutch retailer we had adjusted the software package to meet our demands and our co-operation had been successful.

It was strange that no user group had been founded for this standard package. I was positive about the user group for our Standard Banking System and we discussed the subject with the management of the retailer of the software package. They thought the user group was a good idea and helped us initiate a national user group.

The supplier of the standard package was as first not too keen on the idea but we wanted to have the names of their clients and support systems in order to establish a global user group. We applied some pressure by starting up a national user group and one of the major customers of the supplier became a member. This company supported the user group but did not want to lead the group. It paid off because the supplier decided to support the founding of a global user group.

We proceeded by inviting all the supplier's customers to a first meeting. My partner, the major Telecom Operator, and I had prepared a presentation concerning the set up and the importance of a well-run user group.

As it turned out, all customers were pleased with the initiative and we appointed a Board of Management for the user group. The supplier would sponsor and organise the meetings and take on the administrative work. A date and an agenda were set for the next meeting. I was asked to give a presentation on the developments regarding 'plastic currency' in the Netherlands.

The next meeting was to be held on a ferry between Stockholm and Helsinki. For me it was quite a new experience to try and achieve something amidst men and women who were drinking away happily. I had not realised that alcohol was that important to my fellow travellers.

In spite of the alcohol intake it was a productive meeting and in addition to that we also visited Helsinki. My presentation on 'plastic currency' was a huge success not in the least because I had replaced the word 'plastic' with the word 'rubber'. This added a suggestive character to the story, which was highly appreciated by the male audience.

Again I learned that the combination of having fun and doing business together is highly successful when it comes to solving problems. The supplier usually is the common enemy but also a business partner.

It sounds as if stating the obvious but inviting a relation to an event is a successful and tried and tested way of adding something substantial to a customer relationship. Although the customer is aware of the fact that he is being entertained to improve the relationship and therefore scoring more orders, he is always willing to trail along. No matter what, a customer remains a human being and he will always entertain the thought that he is the one who decides whether to place an order and thereby maintaining a sense of control. But whether that really is the case … ?

Everyone is being used to sell

In order to implement the Information and Automation Plan we had opted for the hardware (PCs) supplied by the number 1 hardware supplier in the world. We used these PCs in our offices not as personal computers but as production computers. These computers ran an application devised by our own company.

The large supplier sold its hardware through retail outlets. We bought the hardware through retailers and our retail representative had been listed as the best the hardware supplier had to offer. Until then we had been satisfied with the supplier and its hardware. We ordered the PCs, usually ten at a time, when we were to open a new branch office. At some point the supplier had decided to stop manufacturing the whole computer but to outsource the assemblage to a low-cost country. As a result we received a number of PCs we could not run our own application on. A major problem as far as we were concerned, since up till then there had never been any problems with running our own application. It had always been one of the main sales arguments of the number one hardware supplier. We had to return the PCs to the retailer without paying the invoice.

Our retailer together with the hardware supplier did not manage to come up with a solution. I got in touch with the hardware supplier's Account Manager. This young man turned out to be useless and thought that we had to rewrite our application to suit their hardware.

That was definitely the limit and I told him in no uncertain terms that I would contact other suppliers in the market until I had found hardware that could run our application. I also said to the Sales Director of the retailer that he should put his money where his mouth was.

My next-door neighbour, a kind and amiable man, was employed at the Technical Services Department of our very own Hardware supplier. We used to get together on a regular basis but hardly ever talked shop. Sometimes my neighbour was forced to entertain business contacts at his home and I could see his brainwashed colleagues in their uniform-like grey trousers and blue blazer sitting in his garden. Also, in their private lives some of them and their families were arrogant. Sometimes I was invited to these gatherings but I never felt at ease surrounded by all that arrogance. Fortunately my neighbours were not like that and his wife always managed to put up a whole show.

One night the neighbour paid me a visit quite unexpectedly. After some general exchanges he got down to business and told me that the management of his company found it hard to swallow that I had decided to purchase new hardware from another company. I was surprised that they had sent my neighbour to do their dirty work for them. I told my neighbour the whole story regarding the problems with the hardware and our own application. He promised he would do something about it and as it turned out our application could run on a number of their PCs but could not on every PC. They arrived at the solution that our retailer would test our application on the PC first before shipping it to us.

I learned that a supplier will sometimes go to great length to keep a customer. Some will go to all lengths.

It's all sales

Every salesperson, including retailers, will have to guarantee continuity. This is always a smart approach to get in touch with other contacts. The question remains why a supplier refuses to adapt, and then all of a sudden changes tack. Did they use every means possible to maintain a good relationship? Did they listen attentively to the problems the customer was facing? The answer is? Well….ask those particular questions.

Not interested in the top job

The Director-general was forced to make some changes to his Management Team. There were a number of reasons but the most important one was the threat the introduction of the Euro posed to the future of our company. And given his age he had to find a suitable candidate to take over from him.

I was still working hard on the implementation of my Information and Automation Plan as a basis and a means of support for the 24 hours a day 7 days a week access to new products and services. Next to that, I was also busy devising integration and a more effective organisation of the process handling of the General and Technical Support Services Department. Fortunately I was still reporting directly to the Director-general, which was very important to me. We worked well together and as long I was reporting directly to him I did not have anything to do with company politics. I was not interested in the schemes of my colleagues. All that changed now that I had joined the Management Team and became more involved in the overall decision-making process of the company.

It was interesting to notice that it became more and more clear that our company depended on the introduction of new products and services supported by automation. Because of that I became increasingly involved in the discussion concerning the future of our company.

All around me others were involved in a power struggle. A new young Bank Director had been appointed but the old Bank Director did not accept him so he did not last very long with the company. I did not respect him either because he pretended to be a director without actually delivering the goods. Add his impudence to that and you have the reason why he was not even liked by his own staff.

A new Bank Director was appointed who was assigned to develop our company into a 24 hours a day operating bank. The Board of Directors, including myself, believed that our banking products would secure the future of our company. The new Bank Director did not pull it off. He did not possess the power and strength required bringing about such an extensive process of change and was not taken seriously.

At one time during an office party he had had a bit too much to drink and had squeezed the breasts of one of the more scantily clad female colleagues. The woman had made quite a fuss about the incident, which eventually led to his dismissal. Many were relieved when he left.

Next, they had also appointed a new Sales and Marketing Director. He was already a wealthy man because of the family fortune and all that was lacking was power. He lived among the rich, who all held important positions. So far he had not been able to achieve this and it hurt.

He also saw himself as a suitable candidate to succeed the Director-general. The only thing he managed to achieve was a new company logo and corporate image. It cost the company an awful lot of money and did not amount to much. He left without having achieved something substantial.

All the newly appointed Directors reproached management for not being given a fair chance to implement real changes. As far as they were concerned the Director-general, together with the Financial Comptroller and the Secretary to the Shareholder's Meeting were the ones to blame. All I could do was offer them a shoulder to cry on but in the end I could only conclude that the Comptroller was 'playing dirty' and was after the position of Director-general.

I tried to remain as neutral as I possibly could. I had no interest in getting involved in these power struggles. As the Automation Director I wanted to stay clear of company politics and only offer support to those who were interested in securing the future of our company. I loved the company, the corporate culture and my colleagues and this motivated me to develop new products and services. This company deserved to overcome its difficulties.

I learned that when it comes to power struggles some people play dirty. I sincerely detested company politics and did not want to get involved. And also company politics lead to a waste of valuable time. The only thing I was interested in was securing the company's future.

It's all sales

Irrespective of the dirty games that are being played, it is also unproductive to engage in activities that do not aim at the company's objectives. Unfortunately it is often the case that differences of opinion or conflicts determine in which direction a company will go; simply because nobody knows how to deal with conflicts and differences of opinion. In cases like this it is always worthwhile to appoint a mediator to determine the underlying reasons for a particular conflict. It is often the case that without mediation all parties involved just continue to muddle on. After all if you have a toothache you go and see a dentist?

Compensating at work

The HR Director had asked me to take on a woman who was somewhat older than my other secretaries. She was hired to support my other two secretaries. The combination of this older secretary and the two younger ones worked out well. They worked well as a team and respected each other. She was happily married and had three children of about the same age as my daughter. She was blessed with a tremendous sense of humour, something that can be expected from a woman born and raised in one of the larger inner cities.

On her first day at the office she was very nervous and when she brought me a cup of coffee her hands were shaking to such an extent that I was afraid the coffee was going to end up in my lap. I immediately got up and made her feel at ease, and later on we had a good laugh about the awkward situation.

She worked part time and was like me an early starter. I got into the habit of getting a cup of cappuccino for her and a cup of regular coffer for myself at the canteen. We would drink our coffee together and talk about life in general and our children. We became firm friends.

I never discussed the problems with my wife with her but I did talk quite often about my daughter. Since my wife no longer showed in interest in raising our daughter I had taken it upon myself to take care of her on my own. And I came to rely on the advice of my secretary when it came to raising my daughter. I hoped that she also valued my advice concerning her children.

One very cold winter morning (it was at least 10 below zero[1]) she arrived at the office in quite a state. On her way from the underground to the office she had been accosted by a flasher who in spite of the cold had shown her his private parts. I phoned the HR Director straight away and he informed the police. He then went to the underground station himself to size up the situation and notify our colleagues.

To take her mind of the incident I went to the canteen to get her an extra cup of cappuccino. After that she felt considerably better and she managed to see the funny side of the incident. A colleague pointed out to her that perhaps it was not a flasher after all but simply someone who had to take a leak and because of the cold had ended up with his male member frozen stiff. Small wonder he had wanted to expose it to her. That did it and now we were all

---

[1] 15 degrees Fahrenheit

laughing. Her husband also saw the funny side of it and also helped her to get over this unpleasant incident.

All the warm and loving stories she told me about her husband and family made me aware of what I was missing out on. I realised how different my life could have been. Sometimes I envied her.

I learned that a warm and loving family is the very basis of our existence. Without love and warmth there is no life, it is the motor of our existence.

It's all sales

In order to be a successful salesperson it is important not to worry about things. Problems will distract and will put you on the wrong track. Everyone has something to worry about but as soon as problems get in the way of doing your job properly it is important to talk to someone about it. A problem that is out in the open will lose some of its impact. Moreover, opinions and advice from others can lead to a different take on things and might help you solve the problem.

Dealing with a difficult financial Comptroller

Until then I had not been very interested in financial matters relating to the company. As far as I was concerned there were already enough bookkeepers, Comptrollers and accountants to make the world go round. I was a specialist in Organisation and Automation and on account of that I possessed unique, specialised knowledge, which was how I earned a living. I hated having to have discussions with the Financial Comptroller about budgets, spending and investments. He always tried to find fault with me because, according to his reasoning, I was the one responsible for spending vast sums of money without getting something tangible in return.

Of course I did understand that the company expected him to behave like this and I did not object to that. What I did not like was the fact that he clearly enjoyed exerting power and that he displayed a blatant lack of respect towards my responsibilities.

Ever since I had joined the Management Team I had to get used to the different role I was to play in the company and I had already shown an interest in the company's finances. The Director-general acted as my coach but I wanted to gain more insight, for I felt I could not trust the Comptroller.

Somewhere along the line I had acquired this strong suspicion that by means of 'clever bookkeeping' he had managed to influence the decision-making process to fit his own needs. Hence my interest in the company's financial background.

My neighbour was the chairman of the indoor leisure centre (sports centre, restaurant, village hall and library) in our village and he was looking for a treasurer for the centre. The financial administration was in the safe hands of an accountant's office. He approached me for the position and I accepted for I thought this would be a good opportunity to put into practice all my recently acquired financial knowledge. And I learned quite a few things on the job. I learned, for instance, how to manage figures and to put them in a certain order according to the desired outcome, as long as it all added up at the bottom of the page.

Because of my new insights I was able to check up on our Comptroller and I did discover that when he did not like a director or when he felt threatened by him he would include certain spending in his report to make things difficult for him. His tactics became abundantly clear when he became responsible for the foreign offices and financial reports were increasingly positive since he had not included spending regarding, amongst others, automation.

As soon as he noticed I was on to what he was doing (I mentioned it during a Board Meeting) he started to change his behaviour towards me. I once more understood that it can be for the good of the company to represent figures in a certain way but 'clever bookkeeping may never lead to personal games to satisfy a Comptroller. The representation of company figures should be a part of corporate policy.'

That is how I learned to assess company finance. The Comptroller was now aware of the fact that I was on to him and changed his behaviour. I did not want his sudden friendship though, for he was not to be trusted.

I discovered that I enjoyed learning on the job and that I was always interested in acquiring more knowledge. I was of an inquisitive nature and that would never stop.

It's all sales

The issue discussed in the story above is better known as 'false statistics'. It is possible to give a wrong impression through misrepresentation of figures. If you wish to accentuate differences, present figures on a larger scale. If it is not in your best interest to accentuate large differences, simply narrow down the scale. Interpretation of figures is also a popular tool for misrepresenting figures. Salespeople are crack mathematicians when it comes to using figures to explain why things did not go according to plan. They use figures to absolve themselves from responsibility.

Selling the 'off-brand banking' concept

I became increasingly involved in the strategy and vision of the company regarding the introduction of new products and services to withstand the threats intrinsic to the introduction of the Euro. The basic Information and Automation Plan had resulted in an infra structure that enabled access to our new products 24 hours a day and seven days a week. Ours was possibly the first bank in the Netherlands to have access to up-to-date bank balance information. Our infrastructure offered sufficient capacity for it to be used by third parties.

In order to convince the management of my company, I had written a discussion paper on the topic of third party use of our infrastructure and in doing so decrease spending. I called my proposal the 'off-brand banking concept' referring to the cut-price and off brand petrol stations in The Netherlands. Of course my proposal was in keeping with the company strategy to sell more banking products in order to withstand the threats. The Board accepted my proposal and I gained permission to start bringing in customers for my 'off-brand' bank.

During a banking seminar organised by our external accountant I met the Director of the bank responsible for government and local council spending. This bank also intended to change its strategy and was looking for new products. During a brainstorming session we arrived at the conclusion that this bank was suited to supply our products to those employed by the government and local councils.

We would enable them to use our infrastructure and knowledge. There was one major problem, though. In order to proceed they would have to alter the company's articles of association. In order to do so they needed approval from the Board of Directors and the Shareholder's Meeting. One of the shareholders was a major bank and those in charge blocked the proposal. The major bank did not want to deal with possible competition and this put a stop to our cooperation.

During another seminar I ran into a director of an association for Physicians and (their) cars. In addition to the products already on offer he also intended to sell banking products to his clientele. It goes without saying that I offered to find out whether my company could be of any help. Together we compiled a business plan and we cooperated successfully on every level. We defined new products and established a new organisation.

As soon as he had finished our business plan our Director-general presented it to the Shareholder's Meeting and the proposal was voted down. Our major shareholder happened to be a large bank and insurance company and they considered the target group more suitable for their own business than ours.

They proposed to continue with our plans and contacts, which is exactly what happened. Yet, our partner did not want to join forces with our major shareholder and that was the end of it. A missed opportunity.

The Director-general and those involved were very disappointed with our major shareholder. All we wanted to do was to introduce new products and bring in new clients in order to withstand the inevitable loss in income inherent in the introduction of the Euro. All our major shareholder could do was to thwart these plans.

Something went definitely wrong here because its shareholder did not support the strategy set out by the company directors.

I learned that the part shareholders play is very important to a company. Sometimes their interests are irreconcilable with the plans of a company. This always leads to major problems. It is of the utmost importance to select shareholders that adhere to the company's policies and strategies.

It's all sales

In sales there are similar situations. Sales Management needs to monitor regularly the development of the product range. The well-known product life cycle should be managed carefully. Also, how products relate to the portfolio of the overall range of products should be taken into account. From this, decisions may emerge to introduce new products and to reposition existing products. A product that has been developed for future revenue needs strong promotion whereas a product that is already successful may need less attention and will still be successful. The salesperson will focus on the existing product (think turnover, bonus etc.) whereas Sales Management will focus on new products.

A deal that could not be won

Slowly but surely my private life had turned into a nightmare. My wife took to the bottle more and more while at the same time trying to hide the fact from me in every manner possible. She used all her wiles to hide her drinking habit from me, but I could always tell from her behaviour. I no longer drank alcohol in my own house. The worst part of the matter was that now she was drunk as well during the day and had made my daughter part of it. We already slept in separate rooms and there was no longer love and harmony in our house. I wanted to wait with divorce proceedings because my daughter had reached puberty and I wanted to protect her from the agony of having to witness her parents going through a divorce.

Now that my wife was drunk so often I could not keep this from my colleagues at work. Occasionally my wife contacted the office and would talk to my secretary on the phone. I had to tell my secretary some details about my private life. This upset her because she had always believed that I had a happy family life. Sometimes I had to leave suddenly during meetings, which of course also attracted attention. I did feel there was some understanding for my situation.

One night after another drunken attack by my wife I could not sleep and I sat on my own downstairs. The sky was clear and I sat there gazing at the stars. The leaves of the two trees in our back garden were rustling quietly in the wind. I started crying and prayed to my God. I was at my wits' end.

After a while I calmed down and my God made it clear to me that most of the basic elements comprising a relationship were no longer present. Nothing positive was left between us and it would be better to end our relationship. Perhaps it was even better for my wife since it was well possible that I was one of the reasons why she had taken to the bottle. The picture that now formed itself in my mind was not encouraging. I pictured myself sitting in a small flat in the big city. I automatically assumed that my daughter would stay with my wife. That is what normally happened in divorce proceedings in the Netherlands.

A couple of days later I arrived home and since my wife was sober I broached the subject of a divorce. I suggested that it might be better for her if we went our separate ways. Even though she did display some anger she also accepted my decision. I promised her I would help her find her feet after the divorce.

The next day I paid a visit to our Physician since he had been her confidant and 'friend' after all. I was invited to surgery that evening and told him that I had decided to end the relationship with my wife. He did not say much but it was clear that he understood why I had reached this decision. 'Easy for him to say' is what I thought at the time.

The next step was much more difficult because I had to tell my daughter. Yet, my daughter made things easy for me and even said that she was relieved because as far as she was concerned I should have divorced her mother three years ago. She also told me that she intended to continue living with me because she no longer felt she could respect her mother and her behaviour. It seemed as if my daughter was happy with my decision.

Well, and then I had to go and tell go my parents. They had not been aware of any problems between my wife and me and I decided not to go into detail since I did not want to discredit my wife too much. They were surprised that I had showed up on my own in the first place and I could not help but cry when I told them about my decision. My parents were there for me, though. I was their son after all, and they supported my decision. I asked them to show some consideration for my wife and they promised they would do so since she was the mother of their granddaughter. Their response generated a sense of warmth and it gave me the energy to start the divorce proceedings.

I learned that some deals cannot be won. As soon as feelings become involved it is difficult to make a deal. In particular when someone is ill or drunk. In this deal, however, all parties lost.

It's all sales

Never make a deal with someone you suspect to be mentally or physically unstable. Under these conditions the deal will be disaster prone and will come back to haunt you. Deals that are made in a bar after having had a few drinks should be verified the next day. Emotions may cause bad decisions.

What people say is not what they do

We had appointed a new Marketing Director and his department grew rapidly. This was essential because we needed new products in order for the company to survive. Time did not work to our advantage. We new exactly what the introduction of the Euro would entail as far as our company results were concerned and the future did not look too bright. Many new, good and lucrative products would be required in order to sustain this blow.

The Marketing Director and the Comptroller had already come to blows and they completely ignored one another. The power struggle was clear for all to see and the 'star prize' was the position of Director-general

One of our successful products was the cashing of cheques. Many of our customers had an overdraught towards the end of the month and would cash a cheque at one of our offices. In this way they would make ends meet until salaries were transferred to their accounts. Our customers accepted the costs of these transactions because they considered the transaction an extra service. The banks saw the benefits of this product and accepted the transactions.

Our marketing department had carried out marketing research regarding, amongst others, this product. They had asked passers-by at Central Stations whether they ever cashed cheques at one of our offices. Most people denied they ever did, when confronted directly because not too many people liked to admit to the fact of having an overdraft. Because of the difficulties between the Comptroller and the Marketing Director the figures for the transactions were not included in the findings that were eventually presented.

When the findings were discussed during the meeting of the Board of Directors the Marketing Director was 'savaged' by the Comptroller who, by simply stating the facts, could prove that this service was actually very lucrative. The defeat suffered by the Marketing Director was complete and left no room for his other, perhaps feasible, recommendations to be discussed.

I learned that it is difficult to assess the behaviour of people. What they say is not what they do and the other way around. People are not honest about matters they are ashamed of and will always be happy to present an accepted opinion because they do not have one of their own. Market research is therefore difficult and relying on it will always be risky.

Information you need to sell has to be reliable. Hence the importance of market research. Yet market research has to abide by a number of rules. The people you include need to be representative for the group you are going to make statements about. Even more important are the questions you are going to ask. Questions touching upon important matters always need to be double checked by means of check questions. These are questions on the same topic but differently worded. By doing so it is easer to assess the value of the answers.

Negotiating a divorce

It felt good that we had decided to start divorce proceedings. I wanted to get it all over and done with as soon as possible in order not to upset my daughter's life too much. We had decided to hire the same divorce lawyer in order to speed up and simplify the whole process.

Our divorce lawyer was a woman and I noticed from the onset that she looked after my wife's best interests. She felt sorry for my wife who was abandoned by this horrible man. The lawyer did not have any background information and was preoccupied with setting up a divorce settlement. This suited me just fine because I wanted to make proper arrangements for my family and accept responsibility because I did feel a bit guilty. And in addition to that, I was grateful to my wife for the 22 years of our lives that we had spent together. Since I was a Bank Director and earned a decent salary the lawyer decided I had to my wife a substantial alimony.

According to Dutch law a man has to pay child support but also alimony for his ex wife if she does not have any means to support her for the duration of twelve years. These years should offer her the opportunity to arrange her own affairs and start earning money to support herself, so the alimony can be reduced. As soon as she earns more than the amount negotiated in the divorce settlement, it is to be deducted from the alimony. The alimony stops as soon as she remarries or starts living together with another partner. When my wife heard of this stipulation she got angry and said that she would do everything within her power to make sure she was financially independent as soon as possible.

Our lawyer had put in a request for all financial details and I had provided them. At her office they had a special computer programme that could determine the exact amount of alimony. The amount specified was definitely too high and when I had a closer look at the print-out it turned out the lawyer had assessed the child support for my daughter considerably lower than it actually was.

Fortunately I had kept good records and I could prove to them what the actual amount was I spent on my daughter. The newly calculated amount turned out to be more than what my secretary earned in a month so my wife would be well off. In addition she was also awarded half of the equity of our house. Once we both signed the divorce settlement the official divorce proceedings would be started and after six months we were officially divorced.

It was not easy to find a new place for my wife. Renting turned out to be impossible in our village so the only option left open was to buy an apartment. Fortunately we managed to find an apartment she liked and that was already agreeably furnished. The couple that hat put the house on the market were to leave for a sunny country and my ex-wife could take over almost every single item of furniture. This suited her just fine and it also meant she did not have to take too many items from my house in which I intended to stay with my daughter. I was also able to obtain a mortgage for my wife through my company.

The day my ex-wife left our house I experienced a true sense of relief. It felt as if a burden was lifted from my shoulders while at the same time it felt as if a daughter had left the house, not my wife. Two days later a neighbour passed by and on entering the living room she said 'now I can feel warmth in this place again'. Her words supported me in the idea that I had made the right decision.

My daughter studied hard and after her mother had left I spent quite some time talking with her. I did not want her to try and take her mother's place. She was a student who should not be running our home. I was responsible for that with the help of our cleaning lady who would come in one morning every week.

So I did all the cooking, I cleaned, did the laundry and ironing and did all I possibly could to make life agreeable for my daughter. At the end of the day there were only a few hours left I could use to relax but it was worth it. I had a job to do and I had to face up to the consequences of getting a divorce.

In spite of all the work my daughter put in, she did not pass her A levels. Due to the problems at home and the divorce she had trouble concentrating. I felt awful about it and also felt I was responsible. My daughter had fallen victim to my behaviour. I had not wanted that to happen but it did anyway.

I learned that as soon as love and warmth disappears from a relationship, all that is left is a business deal. It is important to stay in control of your emotions. The negative impact of a divorce on a child is enormous.

What is a business deal? Can it be an agreement solely based on rational grounds? Well, it is feasible if there is a law that provides for all aspects by means of standards set in advance. This law ensures that the agreement is lived up to. If not, you can ask a court of law to decide upon the matter. But in most cases a business deal is different. This is an agreement made for the benefit of both parties. Both parties get something out of the deal, which is why the deal is maintained. It is therefore essential that both parties add something in order for it to remain worth while. That is why the relationship is so important, it ads something that is not exactly a part of the agreement but that both parties desire.

A 'love story'

My young secretary was an attractive woman. She never seemed to be aware of this but whenever she walked along the corridor she had men eying her up. She liked working for me and she clearly enjoyed the work. Whenever she was enjoying herself she sang songs that we all enjoyed. It is after all pleasurable watching young people being happy.

She was straight forward and honest with me and I felt we knew each other well. We often talked about private matters and work related issues. As far as I am concerned it is always essential to be able to use each other's services. As a manager it is important to form a good team with your secretary. We worked well together and my colleagues knew and appreciated that.

When she first joined the company she had a boyfriend in college. She liked him a lot and whenever she talked about him and her eyes started to glisten and a smile appeared on her face. She also told me he was not Mr Right as far as the rest of her life was concerned. He was not serious enough and was not interested in starting a family and having a future together. Later on she bought a house off a colleague which made her happy and feel pleased with life. She lived as an independent young woman in the city she loved.

One day she told me she had broken up with her boyfriend. She still loved him but since he was not interested in spending the rest of their lives together she had terminated their relationship. She did want to think ahead and have a family of her own. She was sad about the break-up and personally I also thought that her hormones were playing up. Her biological clock obviously had had a say in the matter as well.

In my department we deployed a trainee on a temporary basis. He was an intelligent young man with a mind of his own. In spite of his age he it seemed as if he knew what life was all about. If I argued with him, about his lack of social skills for example he hardly took notice and always wanted to have a final say in the matter.

After his short career in automation he decided to apply for the position of assistant Comptroller, which I arranged for him. I respected him in spite of his lack of social skills for he was good at his job and had this innate desire to win. He was a high potential asset to the company.

My department was located on the fourth flour of the building while the Comptroller and his department were situated on the ground floor. I could not help but notice that this young man all of a sudden had a lot of copying to do and particularly on the photocopier on our floor. For some strange reason the one on the ground floor was always either in use or out of order. We had an external accountant whose catchphrase was 'just do me a copy' which is what probably started it. I was hardly ever around when he did his copying but my secretary was and she also started meeting him when there was no copying to be done.

About six months later my secretary came into my office to inform me about what was already common knowledge. She and the promising young Comptroller were in a relationship together. He had moved in with her and they had big plans for their future together. I told her that her bit of news did not come as a surprise, which in turn baffled her. You now what they say, love makes blind. I was happy for the pair of them because I liked them both and hoped they would be happy together.

Eventually the assistant Comptroller ended up having an argument with the Comptroller. It was only a matter of time before this was to happen, but he left the company and accepted a position as a Comptroller with another bank. Later on he became a member of the Board of Directors. I was proud of him because it was his strength of character that got him the position. And things did go according to plan because they had their little family when my secretary gave birth to a baby boy and they bought a fine house in a pleasant little village.

I learned that it made me happy if my employees were happy. I tried to be a coach as well as a father figure to them. I felt responsible for these young people. They sensed that and it made them feel good as well.

It's all sales

A good balance in life is important. Make sure that you enjoy the work you do. Only do things you enjoy doing. People who have to drag themselves to the office every day or those who are working for the weekend will find that it takes up a lot of energy. It is essential that you are engaged in matters that suit you and not take on the job that earns the most money. Very interesting having the top job with lots of money and status. But if you feel the pressure every day, pressure that soaks up all energy, it might be a good idea to invest somewhere else. Look for a job that suits you so it will not take up all your energy. What you get in return is something you do not think about every day; happiness. What is your reason for being?

Negotiating with two troubled ladies

Openness, honesty and sociable behaviour were very much a part of the culture in my department. The management style I adhered to was based on coaching and my young and smart employees appreciated this. Sickness and absence rates showed that my department compared favourably to other departments. And in particular compared with other companies our score was favourable. Also my department employed more women than the nationwide average.

Employees were an asset to the company and the company was good to them. If there were any problems concerning one of the employees I tried in my capacity of HR manager to intervene. I strongly believed in the relationship between private live and work performance and if one of the employees called in sick I tried to determine what the reason of absence could possibly be. I tried to help them solve their problems whether they were private or business problems. Usually I called round to their house or invited them to dinner so we could discuss their difficulties and try to come to a solution. This is how I tried to get people back to work and usually I succeeded in doing so.

One of our employees, a young, married and insecure woman had been employed by my company for about six months. She enjoyed the work and I saw her gain confidence by the day. She did a good job and slowly but surely her colleagues respected her. She grew in her position and learned a lot. Socialising with colleagues and sharing ideas about married and family live made her more self-assured. She was happy when at work.

After about six months she no longer smiled and I noticed a certain sadness in her eyes. She was no longer happy and called in sick. After about a week I called her and invited her to dinner. I picked her up from her home quite deliberately and on entering the house I noticed that the house was clean and very organised but that there was no warmth or love. It became clear to me what kind of problems she was facing and I was once again confronted with those sad eyes. Over dinner I asked her whether she was happy with her husband. She told me she was not but that she did not dare to raise the matter with him for he had recently lost his brother. In addition to that, her mother truly liked her son in law and she did not want to upset her mother.

I talked to her on a number of occasions and tried to convince her that she was also entitled to happiness. I promised her all the help she needed but she turned the offer down. After a couple of months she resigned. Truly but sadly she was not able to change her life. I experienced this as a personal loss and hoped that one day she would find happiness again.

Another employee also experienced some personal problems. She was living together with her husband and baby son. She was very close to her mother but her mother never really understood what was going on in the mind of her daughter. According to her mother the daughter had to be a stay-at-home mum and give up her job. Her mother also clearly expressed her desire to have more grandchildren. This employee was very emotional and cried easily. She called in sick and I also invited her to dinner.

It turned out she had problems with her husband. She wanted to have another baby but was not convinced that he shared her feelings. She shed bitter tears and decided to ask her husband during the Christmas holidays. Unfortunately Christmas was another six months away, for it was only June. I tried to coach her and teach her to communicate better with her husband. Talking about day-to-day matters was essential. She took my advice to heart, changed her attitude and talked to her husband. It changed their marriage for the better and later on she invited me to dinner as a way to say thank you.

I learned that it is only for the strong to change their lives. Not everyone can or will want to but many should in order to be happy.

It's all sales

It should not really be necessary to change your life. You should try to get back to basics. We were born without problems. During our lifetime we encounter many situations prompted by circumstances, money and power that make us lose track. We talk less so others will not know what is going on in our minds. We do things for the wrong reasons. We maintain situations we should really let go. Who would feel comfortable? Do things you feel good about. If you make the wrong choices, change things. Follow your heart and you will notice that you will reach a sense of 'flow' and that you will find what you are looking for in life: Happiness? And who knows what positive effects this feeling can have on your results …

Selling news in an organisation

We all know who they are. You work for the same company but you never know exactly what they do all day. You cannot tell whether they are productive but they are always engaged in conversation with someone or the other. They like discussing the company and the employees. They want to know everything and pass it on to others. They are an important part of the informal organisation. The informal organisation is important and should be in balance with the formal organisation.

My predecessor, the former head of the Automation Department had been promoted to Head of the General and Technical Serviced Department and in addition to that also to Chairman of the Works Council. I thought it was important that he reported to me and I accepted his considerable role in the informal organisation. I was in the habit of talking to him quite a lot about my plans hoping he would prove to be an ambassador of my plans. And I knew him to be popular with many employees throughout the firm. He was also known as the 'Company Newsletter'.

In some cases it was important to assess how an important decision would go down in the informal organisation before the decision was actually made. Additionally, it was important to prepare people carefully when it came to introducing certain plans. The funny part was that our 'Company Newsletter' could never quite remember who the source of this latest bit of news was after a day of chatting away happily.

I told my deputy about this mechanism and he did not believe me so we decided to put it to the test. The next morning I informed the Newsletter about something I had already told my assistant and my secretary.

Later that day we had a regular meeting in which the 'Newsletter' would take part and as soon as we had reached the A.O.B.[2] part of the meeting the 'Newsletter' could not wait to share the latest piece of news with us. It concerned the bit of information he had picked up from me but he could not for the life of him remember the source.

My deputy roared with laughter which made him turn bright red in the face and then it got very quiet. My secretary had a hard time of it not to burst out in laughter as well. I had to think quickly to come up with a generic joke to save the situation.

---

[2] Any Other Business

I learned to make use of all possibilities to gain loyalty from those employed at the company. I would not abuse this power and did not underestimate the importance of the informal organisation.

It's all sales

In sales it is often de case to introduce proposals at several levels within an organisation or to have 'friends' in the right places. Including the informal circuit will help to come to a more natural decision-making process. Especially people in the lower echelons of the organisation should not be overlooked. They can wield quite a bit of influence.

Not being able to use market information.

This company was the largest mail order company in the Netherlands. They were market leader and since my company was always on the lookout for new products, it made sense that we tried to get in touch with this company to see if there was any room for cooperation.

Our branch offices were in business 24 hours a day and we could perhaps play a part in the payment process (and in particular cash payments) and as a delivery address. At least that is what we anticipated.

Our Sales Director invited me, the Automation Director, to join a meeting with the Sales and Marketing Director of the mail order company. This was a pleasurable meeting for it was proof that automation constituted an important part of the sales process and even a condition for the successful introduction of new products.

The company largely depended on automated systems but the flexibility and the round-the-clock availability of the systems enabled the company to introduce new products swiftly and implement automated interface systems with the suppliers. In those day 'Time to Market' was an often heard phrase but for my company I had changed to 'IT to Market'.

Our first meeting was of an informative nature and both parties left the room with a positive feeling. For me the contacts with the mail order company were a real eye opener, for this company managed to sell its goods in all sections of society. Only, customers did not want to be associated with the company. The customer wanted to stay neutral which is why the company could not act upon the market information they had gathered. It is an interesting phenomenon; having acquired so much knowledge and not being able to act upon it.

The Sales Director asked me what I thought was their best selling item. I automatically thought it had to be towels and bed linen since that was what my ex wife had always ordered from them. But much to my surprise it turned out to be bikinis. According to the Sales Director women did not like buying bikinis in regular shops because they did not want to offer the sales assistant the opportunity to assess their bodies. So the ladies ordered their bikinis through the mail order company, try them on in the privacy of their own homes and would decide whether to buy or return the item. It was fun and interesting to listen to these stories.

Once again I could not help but conclude that consumer behaviour is unpredictable and that thorough market research has to be carried out. And once you have completed such research you cannot always rely on it. Customers need to be treated with respect and information generated through research should be treated confidentially.

In sales it is of the utmost importance to deal with customer information confidentially. Sometimes it can lead to an interesting outcome if you were to use info obtained from one client with another client. But be careful in these situations. The fact that a customer shares confidential information with you is something special. Use it to your advantage while respecting the person who rendered the information at the same time.

Selling through reference visits

We were one of the first users in the world of a standard banking system. In addition to that I was one of the founders of a user group, since my company benefitted considerably from a good and strong user group and in doing so minimise the dependency on the supplier.

The supplier had asked whether they could send their potential clients to my company for a reference visit. Other banks, before taking a decision, were keen on learning from an end user what the product was like and how the supplier dealt with its customers

Our decision to implement a standard software system in the very heart of the bank had not been an easy one. The supplier had to be reliable and act as a partner and the risks for the bank had to be manageable.

The supplier would send just about every potential customer on a reference visit. Nothing I could not handle for I always had a standard presentation at the ready, and I actually enjoyed meeting bankers from all over the world.

I always tried to learn something from their culture and banking habits. The supplying company was not always represented during these reference visits because the customer did not always want them to be present. The supplier relied solely on my qualities as a sales person.

Yet in one week I experienced two rather different reference visits. The first bankers were absolutely dreadful. I did my best to present the system with all the enthusiasm I could muster but it seemed as if they were not interested at all. One of the managers was actually on the brink of falling asleep. That did it for me and with a loud bang I put the cup back on its saucer. Their behaviour was disgraceful and it made me feel uncomfortable, to say the least, and I gabbled out the rest of my story.

Later that week another bank delegation paid us a visit. Their enthusiasm was obvious and they enjoyed the presentation. Their attitude generated energy and we had an open and thorough discussion afterwards. Friendly people that left me feeling well pleased.

I analysed the visits with a colleague who had organised the demonstration visit and together we reached the conclusion that the first bank would not purchase the standard banking system and the second would.

About one month later the supplier's Sales Director contacted me to thank me for my positive contribution to the sales process. He also informed me that the first bank had actually signed the sales contract and that they had apologised for their behaviour. Apparently they had suffered from severe jet lag at the time. He additionally told me that the second bank had opted for the standard system supplied by a competitor.

I learned that henceforth I had to continue asking questions and take stock of what my visitors wanted and why they had decided to visit my company. I also had to learn not to let routine get the better of me. Behaviour does not always indicate what people are going to do.

It's all sales

Before engaging in a sales conversation it is advisable and even necessary to sound out a prospect. First get the feel of a prospect and develop an approach. In this exploratory phase you can determine what the prospect is looking for. So do not engage in a conversation on cars but broach a subject that matters. It creates the basis for a good in-depth conversation.

Selling my knowledge

Electronic payment was booming business. It became increasingly possible to pay with debit or bankcard. Consumers clearly appreciated this service and accepted the fact that the amount was immediately debited to their account. For shopkeepers it was good that they had to have less cash money in their cash registers, which limited the risk of robberies.

My company had played an important part in the introduction of electronic payment. We accepted debit and bank cards in all our branch offices so everyone could pay without any effort for our services and products.

Our minority shareholder was Dutch Railways and we had branch offices located in almost every single train station. It was therefore custom to have regular meetings at all levels of both organisations. We always needed their permission if we intended to introduce new products through our branch offices at the train stations.

In my capacity of Automation Director I was now deeply involved in the development of new products and as a result of that, invited to take part in a meeting with this shareholder. The meetings were always agreeable and towards the end of the meeting one of the participants announced proudly that they had designed a new desk for ticket sales that would be introduced at every train station. They shepherded us in the direction of the trial set-up.

As soon as I saw the trial set-up I was aware that there was absolutely no room on the desk for a pin-code reader. I mentioned it and the Managers told me that they saw no future in electronic payment and had therefore left it out altogether.

I was dumbfounded. Every oil company in the country, the major retail companies, they all had already implemented electronic payment systems. I could not convince them despite my own conviction that given their price differentiation, electronic payment was inevitable. Consumers would undoubtedly applaud the introduction electronic payment since it would dramatically improve the speed of ticket transactions.

On my return from the meeting I informed the Director-general on my findings because he was on good terms with the company. He was also surprised and shared my conviction that they would clearly benefit from the use of electronic payment. He was grateful for my percipience and within a week I was invited by the management of Dutch Railways to give a presentation on the status of electronic payment in the Netherlands. After the presentation the design of the trial desk set-up was changed.

I learned that some major companies do not want to follow the market but want to dictate the market. They are introspective and are not always aware of what is going on outside the company.

Sometimes companies have become so large that they are preoccupied with the internal decision-making process. The number of people these companies employ, the departments and business units are extended to a degree that it is a long and exerting process during which sometimes important developments are overlooked. As a salesperson it is your responsibility to be aware of and point out possible oversights.

My foundations in sales

So far my Information and Automation Plan had led to many positive results for both the company as well as on a personal level. We were now capable of automated transactions with our standard software and had access to a network interface with all offices and in addition to that, we were also able to introduce new products to the market quickly.

The Organisation and Automation department comprised a mixture of experienced and young dynamic employees. I had assumed the position of coach and now devoted my attention to the support of the commercial process of the company. These working surroundings motivated me and I enjoyed going to work every morning. My staff was highly motivated and if there were any technical hiccups they were seen to ungrudgingly and even those who were off duty stayed on until the problems were solved.

Outside the company it was also noticed what we had achieved because the implementation of standard software systems and outsourcing when possible without developers was not common in the automation industry.

The young employees on my team increased their knowledge and therefore their potential. They were usually in a relationship and in some cases they even had children. They would often discuss private matters and exchanged opinions on how to deal with problems. Not always their parents understood what they were doing and they were looking for support and understanding. We operated like a close family. And since I was responsible for HR matters, I tried to help whenever I could.

One of my employees had noticed my positive attitude and approach to life. Like me he always arrived early at the office and I used to talk to him quite often because as far as I was concerned he operated as my 'ears and eyes' on the work floor. He usually pointed out to me any possible difficulties. Prevention is always the preferred option and because of him I could respond adequately.

One morning he asked me outright why I always had this positive approach. He envied me and wanted to copy it. By simply asking me that question he set in motion a whole process of thought. I had never thought about it myself. Where did it stem from? Where did I find my strength? He wanted us to meet because he was intent on finding out. We agreed to have dinner a week later.

Over dinner he kept asking me questions about what he referred to as 'my secret'. He wanted to know all there is to know about me and he really made me think about what 'made me tick'. I honestly did not know, which was unfortunate because self-knowledge always comes in handy. That night I could let him into the ´secret´.

But he had set things in motion. I immersed myself in spiritual matters, got involved in readings, attended haptonomy sessions, learned to meditate and read all I could lay my hands on about what made people tick. I also became aware that I prayed to my God every night and I would open my mind to Him and thank Him for everything I was allowed to do.

I meditated every night and I would never skip it, no matter where I was. I learned to give without wishing to receive and HE made me learn to enjoy every second of life since you cannot change the past and we do not know the future. I had uncovered the foundations of what I emanated naturally. My faith was my strength.

I learned to get to know myself better, which made me a better coach for my staff

It's all sales

The basis in the sales process is positive outlook on life and to enjoy dealing with people. My faith always helped my to believe in a positive outcome no matter what I do. That does not mean that you will win every deal. That is not possible but you can learn something from every deal, whether you win or lose.

Evaluation of my personal sales process

After the divorce had come through I had to take care of my daughter. Next to my job I had to take care of shopping, cooking, cleaning, laundry, ironing and looking after the garden. We still employed a cleaning lady for half a day per week but that did not suffice. I had agreed with my daughter that she should not try to take over the role of her mother but that she had to lead her own life as a student and was responsible for her own room only. Nevertheless, the cleaning lady did feel a bit sorry for my daughter and helped her out occasionally without me knowing (or at least, that is what they thought).

My job took up a lot of time and energy and I had to plan my private life carefully. There was hardly any time left for the fun things in life. My whole salary was spent on paying for my wife's alimony, the mortgage, the upkeep of my house, shopping and my daughter. I had nothing left to spend on my own interests. I accepted this and was not at all interested in going out or having another woman in my life. I was deeply hurt and I wanted to ascertain what I had done wrong in order not to repeat the mistakes later on in life. The only bit of fun left to me was the bi weekly game of indoor soccer.

On Sunday afternoons I usually had a couple of hours to myself. I could sit down somewhere quietly, keep up with my trade journals and listen to my favourite music. I noticed I was detached from the music. Everyone around me had pegged me down as the strong man with a positive attitude to life and no problems to speak of. I always had to be there for my daughter and my staff.

Also my ex-wife called me regularly to help her out with her financial affairs and other matters. I had lost a number of friends we had had in common because they did not know how to deal with the changed situation. I felt increasingly lonely and alone. I had to be strong, though. There was no doubt in my mind about that.

Sometimes when I was listening to my favourite music I could not muster up any positive feelings about myself. I was sad and it was not quite clear why. Why did this have to happen in my life? All the emotional and material investments I had made in my relationship had only left me with a beautiful daughter. That was all that my relationship had brought me. Why had I stayed in the relationship since I was very well aware of the fact that it was no longer a good relationship? All these questions brought about a process of acceptance, whether I liked it or not.

I had to go on for my daughter's sake. She was worth it all and she needed me, but for the rest of it nothing mattered. I had a very rough time of it, yet slowly but surely I gained enough strength to get back on my feet again and approach life with a positive feeling once more.

I did have to change my life. But how and what did it take? It was not clear to me and it was easier said than done. For so long I had always been the giving one and now I would have to become the recipient. An enormous change in my life. I was not sure whether I would ever be able to accomplish this without the help of others.

It was, however, crystal clear to me that my home was a safe place again. No longer was there a drunk and screaming woman around. I felt peace and quiet whenever I arrived home. Emotionally I felt liberated from those horrible days and I started to enjoy these quiet moments more and more.

It was clear to me that I had to live my own life and that I had to change. I had not yet figured out how, but I was ready and willing.

It's all sales

Customer is king. But not at every price. A salesperson will come across customers, who demand a disproportionate amount of attention. These particular customers end up in talking about their company incessantly and keep on broaching subjects they want to discuss with you. It is, of course, pleasant if a customer acknowledges you as a supplier, but these customers are too demanding and take up too much time and energy. It is good practice to be very clear to your customer. Try to determine why he demands so much from you and try to advice him on how he can learn to spend his time more effectively. How to manage my customer ...

Selling a sex change

The external consultants who helped us develop the unique applications for our offices came to us through a preferred supplier. The external employees were treated as equals. We made no difference and that was appreciated.

It was quite obvious that one of the external programmers was not happy. He spent a lot of time with the secretaries and talked to them about his problems. He felt at home in our department and enjoyed working with us. He was completely dissatisfied with himself and my secretary told me that he felt as if he was more feminine than masculine and that he was actually in the process of having a sex change operation. He talked quite openly about the matter and he had asked my secretary to inform me. He obviously needed some time off for the operation but after it was finished he wanted to return to our department.

I discussed the matter with my secretaries and they advised me that it would be beneficial to him/her if he/she were to return in a safe environment. They were convinced that the colleagues would accept his choice and would learn to deal with it. We had to accept his choice, which is what happened. My secretaries visited him at the hospital and after a few weeks he returned to my department as a woman and continued working as a programmer.

We had informed all those in the department and had asked for some understanding and it was great to see how they all accepted the new situation. I did realise that it was difficult for her to be a daughter to parents that raised her as a son and for the parents to accept this. That was the reason we supported her as much as we could because hers was not an easy battle. Hopefully she was happier as a woman.

Event though we accepted the colleague's choice, in every-day situations it was not always easy to deal with the changes. She now, for instance, made use of the ladies´ toilets whereas for us men it was not easy to work out whether we should compliment her on her looks or not. No, this was not an easy process for anyone.

After her contract had run out she said goodbye and thanked us all for the support she had experienced. This was good to hear and I was once more proud of my staff and the way they had tried to deal with this change.

I learned that good working conditions and an agreeable working culture will lead to more sociable and respectful behaviour towards others. The positive energy helped people to believe in themselves and to take important personal decisions. Everybody benefitted from such pleasant conditions.

Also in sales the atmosphere within the team can have a major influence on results. When salespeople get along with each other and offer help and advice to their colleagues it will take much less energy to get good results. Sales Management is responsible for good working conditions and they ought to know that inspiring surroundings helps to generate good results. It is important to remind ourselves of this every once or a while. And not wait until the atmosphere is troubled.

Buying a standard software package in one week

My Information and Automation policy for the company was based on buying and implementing standard software. We had already implemented a standard banking system, a standard financial administration system and a standard system for processing electronic payment transactions. The successful implementation of standard software was based on the willingness of top-level management to adapt the organisation and processes. The willingness was certainly present within my company and was based on positive experiences with acquired and implemented standard software.

One of our most successful and profitable products was our foreign currency exchange service. We were market leader in the Netherlands and had nothing to fear from global competition. In order to expand this line of business we had appointed a new manager. He had compiled a business plan and a part of this plan was that he needed a good automation system in order to support the processes. He asked me for support for his plans and he did not intend to waste any time.

One of my organisation/information analysts carried out preliminary research into the possibilities in the market focus on finding a standard software system. There was only one supplier who could provide a reliable and unique system. There was only one 'slight' drawback; this company was located on the other side of the world at a flying distance of 24 hours.

I talked it through with the Director-general and the new Departmental Manager. The Director-general wanted to have access to the system as soon as possible because he also saw the potential future benefits. At the same time he wanted to limit the costs and implementation as much as he could and on top of that he also wanted to invest in this new system in that particular fiscal year.

His proposal was that together with the organisation/information analyst I would visit the supplying company for the duration of a week. We would take an extended wish list with us and we would be ready to advise the company by the end of that week. I also asked whether we could bring the departmental manager along but that proved to be impossible. They would rely on our advice. Even thought we had discussed our list extensively with all those involved prior to our departure we still felt burdened down with responsibility.

It was a demanding trip. We had designated some time for sight seeing but we worked long days all week. We spent a lot of time with the supplier and went on reference visits. It was exhausting and on our flight back we reached a conclusion and were ready to advise the Board of Directors.

Our advice was positive because the standard system met most of our requirements and also the interface with other systems was defined and feasible

Implementation turned out to be more complex than anticipated. The main problem was that a number of end-users had not seen the system before implementation and therefore had the feeling this system was 'rammed down their throats' by their new Manager and the Automation Department. It took a lot of effort to clear the air and to convince the end- users. Fortunately we were able to overcome most of their objections by the fact that the standard system actually worked and proved its worth over and over again.

I learned that when it comes to buying and implementing standard software it just takes time in order to familiarise the end-users with the system and to engage in a solid selling process. At the end of the day it is the end-user who needs to work with the system and the end-user has to accept it.

It's all sales

When you sell a product that is going to be used by others, it can be useful, even essential, to include the end-users in the process. Management can otherwise be forced to reverse their decision. Yet, if you include the end-user in the decision-making process make sure the end-user offers valid advice. Once when I tried to introduce a new brand of coffee creamer the catering lady voted against the proposed brand. She did so as it later turned out because the new brand did not offer trading stamps.

Selling warmth and love

My daughter and I had stayed on in our large house. My daughter enjoyed being in a familiar environment, surrounded by her friends. There were not too many changes to her life now that her mother was not around any more and she also found some peace and quiet. I had to go on a foreign business trip for a week and I had arranged for the neighbours to keep an eye on things since my daughter intended to stay home on her own.

In that period of time my parents had sold their self-built home and had rented an apartment. They were already of an age and my father (75) had finally decided to stop working altogether. My father contacted me at some point because there was a delay in the completion of their apartment and they had to find somewhere to stay for six weeks. I suggested that they would come and live with my daughter and me for those six weeks. There was ample space available and my parents accepted the offer. They would arrive in the weekend I was due to return from my business trip.

My daughter was at home when her grandparents arrived and she made them feel welcome and at home. And on my return from my business trip we discussed 'house rules' in order to avoid problems. But it all went harmoniously. The grandparents loved my daughter and they enjoyed having her around. They had dinner with her, spoiled her and went on fun outings with her. My daughter in return loved her grandparents and enjoyed all the attention that came her way. She did tell me that the Grandparents took up a lot of her time so that she could devote less attention to her homework.

My father wanted to learn from me how to run the home and what it involved like for instance shopping, cooking cleaning, laundry, ironing etc. I had become very proficient in all these tasks since I had no alternative. Years later when he had to look after my mother he told me I was the one who had taught him how to get by. He was determined to remain independent of others.

After about six weeks the grandparents moved in to their new apartment. My daughter and I had enjoyed having them around and the bond between my parents and myself had been strengthened but also the bond between them and my daughter. We had an enjoyable time of it and we missed the 'oldies' because now the house was quiet again.

A week after my parents had left, my daughter received her school report card. She did not expect good results but much to my surprised she had scored 1 to 2 points higher for every subject. My daughter was pleased with the results and it goes without saying I was proud of her. It made me think, though.

It dawned upon me that the warm and loving atmosphere created by her grandparents had generated these good results. My daughter had been without love for too long. Her mother could not give it since her own parents had never loved her. My ex wife had never realised this and only asked for love and attention not being able to give anything in return. Of course I gave my daughter all the paternal love I had in me, but a child needs maternal love. Unfortunately it had never been around and now my daughter would certainly never experience it.

I became increasingly interested in the reason for our existence and the spiritual world around us. I spent a lot of time reading about these matters and the books by Wayne Dyer were real eye openers. The books held up a mirror to myself every time which turned out to be a valuable process and I learned to enjoy life once more. Every day was a beautiful day as far as I was concerned.

I learned that warmth and love are what makes the world go round. No life without love and warmth. Of course I wanted to receive those but in order to do so I had to change and learn to receive and not only give.

It's all sales

In order to be a good salesperson it is essential to feel good about yourself. The positive forces emitted by that basic attitude are immeasurable. Do not assert a positive attitude toward yourself for opportunistic reasons but let it stem from outside yourself. Somebody with a positive attitude towards life is better equipped to achieve positive results than somebody who is burdened by problems. A positive attitude is something that you can give but can also take.

Playing at being manager does not sell

This banker had learned his trade with a large bank. He had now been appointed Bank Director with our bank. His predecessor had implemented the Standard Banking System and I did not have a lot of dealings with him. The bank projects were based on minor adjustments and maintenance and for the larger projects (new products) I could turn to the operational Bank Director who reported to the new Bank Director.

All my time and energy was devoted to the introduction and implementation of new products that were usually based on the present functional and technical infrastructure. Securing the future of my company once the Euro had been introduced was my top priority.

The Director-general had to be admitted to hospital for knee surgery and for the duration of his hospitalisation I had to report to the Bank Director. I noticed straight away that he did not know the first thing about Automation. I missed the Director-general who was always willing to be my sparring partner. This Director did not know what he was talking about. Sometimes he took decisions, which were downright laughable. He could get very excited about minor incidents but the important issues he totally ignored. I noticed that virtually everybody in the organisation disliked him and did not take him seriously and I soon joined that club. I decided to take my own decisions and to try keeping him from making major mistakes. I would only ask for his input on minor decisions. And even with those he managed to take exactly the wrong decision.

When a project for the bank was completed successfully, it was our habit to organise an extended drinks session paid for by the company to be held at our regular cafe. We had once more completed a project and it was time to head for the cafe so I asked the Bank Director for permission to organise it.

He asked me how much this would cost and when I named the sum he said it was too expensive. He had to keep an eye on expenditure and he had a better idea since he did share the notion that those who had worked on the project should be rewarded. His idea was to order a case with two bottles of wine.

I had to accept his decision and I ordered the cases of wine from my local wine shop. When we received the bill it turned out that the bill was twice as high as the cost of an average drinks sessions at our local cafe. We had known this from the start because not everybody was always able to make it to our drinks sessions and now everybody was rewarded with a case of wine. The Bank Director signed the bill and seemed to have forgotten everything about his decision. Even taking simple decisions was beyond him.

95

After a couple of months the Bank Director was fired. He was obviously not the right man for the job. And he certainly was not capable of securing the company's future.

I learned that fighting ignorance took a lot of negative energy. I enjoyed working together with people at the same or a higher level.

As a salesperson you cannot choose the people you have to deal with. Yet, you still have to do business with this person. This requires a lot of empathy and flexibility from the salesperson. A good salesperson will always look for a point of departure in order to interest the customer. Sometimes it will not work no matter what you do. A customer remains distant and is not willing to deal with you as an equal. If that is the case, limit yourself to providing information. A reluctant customer takes up a lot of energy.

How to sell innovation

For the introduction and development of new products it was important to visit market trend related seminars. One of the speakers at one of these seminars was a professor who, next to his work at the University, was also a member of the Board of Executives of our shareholder Dutch Railways. He was a gifted and humorous speaker and it was always a pleasure listening to him.

He once told us the story of the train timetable. The timetable was the 'Bible' to those employed by Dutch Railways. All sorts of important information necessary for those who worked for Dutch Railways could be found in this 'Bible'. Therefore the timetable had been proclaimed sacrosanct.

The professor had asked one of his students to enter the timetable data into a PC. This very clever student had entered all the data into a programme on a fairly standard PC in three months time. With this simple computer programme it was easy to determine at what time a train would depart, arrive and so forth. The entire timetable had been included in the computer programme. Since the programme was fairly straightforward it was also easy to copy and therefore readily available to anyone who had access to a computer. In those days the number of PCs was on the increase. Internet was still in its infancy.

The programme had been finished in three months time but it took the Dutch Railway employees three years to introduce it and accept it. Dutch Railway staff would be seated behind their desks with the timetable on their lap opposite their PCs checking whether the programme offered the correct information. They refused to believe that their 'Bible' could have been converted into a computer programme. It took three years of hard work to convince them that the programme actually worked. It took additional time to prepare the programme for consumer usage.

The professor ended his plea with a piece of sound advice. Companies bound for innovation should first make sure the organisation is ready for change in order to be able to accept the consequences of the pending changes.

I learned that I enjoyed being part of innovative projects and transform a company. It had always been one of my main challenges and I had always been good at selling changes.

Also for customers it is not matter-of-course to accept change. Do not underestimate the effects that can be brought about by changes to products, ordering procedure or in providing information. The client could easily think that a particular service is no longer available to them. Always think when implementing changes about the consequences of these changes for your customer.

Positive energy for a winner

Sometimes I was asked to take on employees for social reasons. I usually did not raise any objections because it solved the shortage of manpower. Usually these people were highly motivated and by hiring them I would not have to engage in a long recruitment process.

This young man I was asked to employ was a special case. He was suffering from thyroid gland cancer and had to receive quite intensive treatment. As a result of this he was all skin and bones. He was raised in a family with three brothers in a small village close to the big city. The culture in the village was typical; hard-working people without time for emotions. If you did not have a job you did not count. This young man was unemployed and on top of that he was seriously ill. He grew up in these cold surroundings in which the mother ruled the family with an iron hand. He was ashamed of the fact that he could not get a job and that made him feel even worse.

Since he had joined our department it was clear he felt better because of the friendly surroundings. Everybody treated him as an equal and soon he became a specialist in PC network systems and was also appreciated for his knowledge. This meant the world to him, for now he was valuable to others. This had an effect on his health. He wanted to conquer this horrible disease and was determined to achieve this.

Sometimes I talked to him privately and he would tell me about his illness. He could always contact a professor at the hospital whenever he did not feel too well. The professor also informed him if a new medicine was to become available. He was always given this new medicine and sometimes acted as a guinea pig. That did not bother him because above all he wanted to overcome his illness. He deserved to win and to live.

Sometimes he had to be admitted to hospital and I would visit him. I would take the laptop computer with me and said to him that whenever he felt like it he could do some work on the laptop. We never registered him as sick. He was important to the department and everybody had to be aware of this. He would do some work in his hospital bed and the fact that we needed him was something he needed to experience.

During one of my hospital visits his mother and father were also present. His mother talked all the time, expressing the fact that she had to suffer so much because of her son's illness. She complained about her son and managed to draw all attention to her. I hated this, looked at my employee and winked at him. He winked back and we knew we understood each other without putting things into words.

I seized the opportunity to tell his parents how important their son was to the company and I could tell that he appreciated my efforts. When I left he tried to express his gratitude by holding onto my hand just a bit longer.

He was crazy about his car and we teased him no end about his devotion to it. We would jokingly accuse him of even washing the underside of his car. His car was his sanctuary. We were pleasantly surprised when at some point he announced he was engaged to be married. He invited us all to the wedding and we made a big deal out of it and even did a sketch. Now his life had turned to normal, just like the lives of his parents and the others in his village.

After a while a large part of my department was dismantled. He was not part of the deal that was made and I arranged with the new and unfeeling Director-general that he would keep the same status and support as before. He promised but I could tell from the look in his eyes that he was not likely to keep his promise.

A year later the employee got in touch once more. He told me that he was seriously ill and could no longer work. The company only allowed him sick pay and he asked me to come and visit. I felt sad because I could tell he was fighting a losing battle. It was to be my final visit. When I sat down in a chair next to his bed surrounded by his family and I could not help noticing his mother drawing all attention to her once more. He lay there looking skinny and ill. Nothing was left of the young man we had celebrated with on his wedding day, but I treated him as I had always done.

At some point I felt that he was looking at me intently. When I looked at him I could see a look in his eyes, a look that said thank you. I looked back at him with all the love and warmth I had in me. When I left I gave him a long and firm handshake. Two days later I received the message that he had passed away.

I could not make it to his funeral because it was on the day I was to move into my new apartment. Later on I did not regret the fact that I could not attend for as it turned out his mother had once again taken centre stage. At least I had not been forced to witness that.

Again I learned what positive energy could do for people. It can be the difference between life and death.

When do you function best: when you receive a compliment or when you are reprimanded. It should be obvious that you will feel better with a positive approach. Still, when we only give each other positive feedback it will backfire. In other words, try to find the right balance between compliment and correction. A customer can be corrected occasionally; he will appreciate you more than if you continually agree with him.

Selling independence to my daughter

In the meantime my daughter had been accepted at the School for Business Administration and Economics. She enjoyed the subject and enjoyed everything life as a student had to offer. Despite my wishes she did decide to play a more important part in the running of our home and take over some of her mother's tasks. I was not pleased with this turn of events but I could not always avoid it.

My secretary had decided to move in with her boyfriend. She lived in small but comfortable house in the city centre and had enjoyed living there. Even though she had decided to share a house with her boyfriend she was not quite ready to sell her home but wanted to rent it out furnished, for she did not know whether living together would work out. If it did not, she could always move back into her beloved house.

I inquired whether it was possible to rent the house for my daughter. She thought it an excellent idea because this solution offered security for the future. I also asked her for an option to buy the house at market price if the house was ever put up for sale. It was good for tax purposes to purchase a house for a studying child. She also liked this idea.

To me it was important that my daughter and only child would be able to get by in the big city. My aim was for her to become financially and emotionally independent. She could after all not rely on her mother or brothers or sisters. She would have to do it on her own. Independence was my dream for her future.

I had to tread carefully with my daughter. I did not want to give her the impression that I wanted to 'get rid' of her. Independence would do her good and it would be selfish to have only my own interests at heart because once she left the house I would be left to my own devices and it would be terribly quiet without having her around. The last thing I wanted was to upset her.

I waited for the right moment to broach the subject of our future. But from the onset she joined in the conversation enthusiastically and when I told her about my secretary's house she was pleased no end because she knew and admired my secretary. I promised her I would not sell our house for another six months so if it did not work out she could always come back home. She would, of course, have to keep her job because she did have to pay rent to me.

My daughter had a wonderful time living in her own little house in the big city. She would go out with her friends and as a proud father I saw her moving into adulthood. Yet she did call me every month to let me know she had transferred the rent to my bank account. She was hoping I would tell her not to. I did no such thing but advised her instead to pay by direct debit. It was not easy to be tough with her but it was for her own good.

The only problem my daughter and I could not solve was the mice. The mice would have a ball right above her head in the space between the ceiling. Her house was squeaky clean, but the mice apparently needed her ceiling to travel to the next-door neighbours. We never managed to solve the rodent problem.

I learned that I was always concerned with other people's best interests and not my own. As far as my daughter was concerned that was, of course, not a problem. One thing I was very clear about do not mess with children. I could not possibly respect anyone who was not good to children. Yet I had to learn to look after my own interests.

It's all sales

What can be more beautiful than to witness other people's happiness? People with the right approach to life are able to experience other people's happiness. They are even willing to sacrifice some of their own happiness. Every person needs to fight for his own happiness and be ready and willing to accept it. You can only bring happiness if you experience happiness yourself..

Dealing with a shovel attack

Our main office was situated on the outskirts of a major city, right in between other office buildings and offering easy access to staff and business traffic. The business traffic mainly consisted of money transport vans, which would take cash money (mostly foreign bank notes) to and from our offices and customers to the main office and the other way around.

The highly secure unit carrying out cash transactions was situated on the first floor of our main office. Our main office had four floors with two wings each. My department comprised the entire fourth flour and my office was situated right in the middle of the fourth floor. From my office window I had a splendid view overlooking the parking lot and of course the very location of my office made me both the physical and the spiritual centre of my department.

I had always enjoyed having an early start (7.30 a.m.). Starting early enabled me to go through the mail at leisure, prepare for meetings and assign work to the secretaries. And at this time of day I made sure the door to my office was always open and those who wished to talk to me knew where to find me. Some of my staff followed my example and started work early so they could avoid rush hour traffic.

One Friday morning I was disturbed whilst going through my morning routine by a loud, banging sound. When I looked outside I was just in time to witness a hydraulic shovel crashing the main gate to our office. That very same shovel was now attempting to drive a hole in the outer wall of the building with its bucket, right where the highly secure cash department was situated. I also noticed a man carrying a firearm standing on the shovel, his face covered by a balaclava. I immediately notified the doorman and he told me he had already called 911 and the police were on their way.

I realised other dangers presented itself for they might decided to use explosives to blow a hole in the outer wall. I decided to take action and make sure my people were safe. I asked them to come to the wing of the building that was not under attack and I told them to stay clear of the windows. Fortunately the other wing was under attack but I still felt powerless and angry. One of my female employees went back to the other wing to collect her handbag. I got (unreasonably) angry with her.

It took an awful long time before the police arrived and I found it difficult to contain my impatience. There was nothing I could do. I could not play the hero and I found it hard to deal with feeling powerless. Fortunately the attack failed because the shovel could not destroy our outer wall. The attackers did manage to leave with a get-away car. Nobody got hurt.

I learned to control my feelings and actions and to wait. It went against my nature and afterwards I hated myself for not taking out a fire hose or something and blast the bad guys from the shovel. I would have loved playing the hero, but could not because of my position.

It's all sales

In keeping with the story above is the situation surrounding sales. You have done absolutely everything to prepare the order and you have informed your customer into detail. All he needs to do is to say yes. And then it gets quiet. Did a competitor manage to get the order? Was the proposal not good enough? I had done everything to prepare properly. There is nothing you can do but allow the customer the opportunity to think things over. It is a sense of powerlessness that every salesperson will experience at one time or the other .

Selling a corporate bank

Our main shareholder was a large financial company comprising a conglomerate of different financial companies. They acquired and sold financial establishments in their capacity of Investment Company. Every subsidiary sold its products under its own label. They would discuss possible forms of cooperation but none of it ever came to pass because all the individual companies wanted to remain independent.

Our shareholder had decided to establish a corporate bank. They already owned a savings and a retail bank but customer demand for corporate banking was on the increase. In order to meet this need they had appointed a banker who was familiar with all the ins and outs of corporate banking. He was assigned to establish a corporate bank from scratch. He was an intelligent man and he knew that good automation infrastructures were of essence to a corporate bank. He had carried out an internal survey, which had made clear that my company had a standard banking system that would be perfectly suited for what he had in mind.

I was invited to join the Steering Committee initiated by the major shareholder to establish the corporate bank. I considered the invitation quite an honour because I always had to 'fight' against the management of the Automation Department of the major shareholder. Until now they had never shared my belief in standard software and in the past they had tried to take over my computer centre. Was this a personal victory? I was aware of the many internal political dangers I would encounter. Anyone who was anyone in banking knew that the Management of the Automation Department of the major shareholder was very powerful and if they were to decide that something was not in their best interest, they would block it.

Our banking system had to be linked up to the legacy system of the major shareholder and so the Management of the Automation Department of the major shareholder had appointed one of their staff to take part in the Steering Committee. It was impossible to work together with this delegate because instead of coming up with solutions for a problem he would add at least seven additional problems. He never solved anything and never carried out his action points. Before he would speak he always prepared a roll-up, light it and would not do anything before he had finished his smoke. In doing so he would protract the project enormously. The Director of the Steering Committee seemed to be powerless to do anything about it.

After about three months the project came to a standstill. Our major shareholder had taken over a mid-size corporate bank and there was no longer a need to establish its own corporate bank. All our hard work had been in vain and we were not too pleased about that.

A couple of years later I ran into the representative of the major shareholder again and he asked whether he could have a word with me in private. During our conversation he apologised because, as he explained, management had instructed him to slow down and sabotage the process. Since I had already suspected this, the truth did not come as a surprise. I accepted his apologies. Why not? It was in the past, all water under the bridge.

I learned again that automation should be there for the benefit of the commercial process in a company. Fortunately that is how I always acted with regard to my company. In my opinion automation should stay well clear of company politics.

It's all sales

In sales you sometimes come across people who oppose you. They only have one goal and that is not to buy anything. In itself these people can be good sparring partners but mostly they are quite frustrating. You can get frustrated and start doubting yourself. My advice: try to confront your opponent with his behaviour. Why are you treating me this way? After you have done this, you will notice a change in behaviour from your opponent.

Love sells

My daughter had moved out of our house and now lived in the big city where she went to school and worked. I supported her financially with her rent, pocket money and a monthly clothing allowance.

One day she phoned me at the office and told me that she had secured a trainee position with a bank. She also informed that she had a bit of a problem because she now had to get a business suit and she was not able to afford that out of her clothing allowance. A business suit was too expensive. She continued by inviting me to come with her on her shopping trip.

It goes without saying that I understood the business suit predicament. I realised that I was about to witness my daughter's first steps on the 'business scene'. Her request also made me feel a bit sad because under normal circumstances her mother would have been the one to join her on this shopping trip. Well, since that was not possible I decided to turn the whole enterprise into one big celebration and I decided to take the afternoon off from work to go shopping with her. We went to a shopping mall we both liked and frequented.

On our arrival at the shopping centre we headed straight for a ladies fashion shop and I explained to the (somewhat elderly) sales lady what my daughter was looking for and why. Apparently the sales lady found it rather special that I had joined my daughter and tried her utmost to sell everything she could and even had one of her colleagues join in. My daughter clearly liked all the attention and it all turned into one big event.

My daughter enjoyed it all and we chose two business suits with matching blouses. When I paid with my credit card the sales lady said to me that my daughter definitely needed shoes and tights to go with the suit. She accompanied us out of the shop and pointed out the shops where we might find the desired articles.

We took her advice and the same procedure followed in every shop we entered. I suggested buying a long coat for her to wear with the suit and we also managed to by a suitable coat. My credit card was definitely used a lot that day. Heavily burdened with all her shopping she finally decided she would need a brush to remove fluff and dust from her newly acquired coat. So we set out to buy a clothes brush which cost exactly 1 Euro. This time my daughter paid, she even insisted.

By that time we had bought everything we could possibly think of and we decided to celebrate the successful outcome of our shopping spree with dinner in a restaurant.

Two days later I received a thank-you card from my daughter. She thanked me for everything and suggested jokily that we should go shopping more often. Great! And I felt good about the whole enterprise.

I learned that I enjoyed watching my daughter grow up. I was immensely proud of her. By selling my daughters 'predicament' to all the shops my daughter received special treatment because sales staff could relate to her situation.

It's all sales

Not only the sales lady in the first shop was an excellent salesperson and made the most of the situation. But how about the daughter? She managed to create willingness with her father to help her out. More than that, he actually enjoyed it.

Developing a product quickly

We now used the new Standard Banking System to make all our banking products available through the main office and our branch offices 24-hours a day and seven days a week. All those involved were pleased with the banking system. Yet a new challenge arose. We had to offer new products to the market in order to increase our market share and counteract the threats posed by the introduction of the single currency (Euro).

The supplier of the Standard Banking System had approached me with the request to host reference visits from potential customers. I had agreed to this because to me it was important to have a strong supplier with many customers. My company would benefit from this. So I was in the habit of giving presentations to other bankers regarding the flexibility of our Standard Banking System because it was fairly simple (just adapt a few tables) to include new products. There was one problem, though; I did not have any samples to support my statement.

As it turned out, one of shareholders, Dutch Railways, was developing a product together with a large bank that would enable travellers to take out a loan to buy an annual rail travel card. They had already been working on the development of this project for about a year and were ready for the trial runs.

We informed the Director-general of what we had discovered and he got in touch with the shareholder straight away. He reminded them of the fact that we also offered banking services and that according to the principal agreement our company was to provide all financial services for our shareholder. He did not know anything about it of course but he did get back to us and offered us the opportunity to make a bid as well, but we would have to be able to process the product within one month's time. If we were able to pull that off, we would very likely be awarded the contract since we had branch offices in almost every central station anyway.

Together with the operational manager of the bank we put together a project plan in no time and set to work immediately. This was an opportunity we could not afford to miss out on. The project was awarded top priority status and we managed to develop this product in one month's time by parameterise the standard banking system, setting up the administrative organisation, test the whole course and implement it. And as a result we were awarded the contract.

We were very proud of our achievements; especially because the outcome of our hard work proved that standard software could fully support our product development. "IT to the market".

I learned that sometimes it could take quite a while to make a dream come true. But if in the end it all works out well, it is very satisfactory.

It's all sales

It is essential to keep an eye on market developments. There are often sales opportunities within organisations with several units even if it is not a matter of course that a subsidiary will buy products from you. Also in cases like this you will have to go through the entire sales process. Skipping a few steps along the way because take getting the order for granted can backfire.

My soul is not for sale

Moving from a rather large house to a small apartment is not easy. Many items had to be sold and even then there were still too many things left. The good thing was that I was alone and therefore did not have to compromise. But I will not easily forget the day I moved because I was on my own and I felt lonely and sad. All these boxes I had to unpack, it was not easy.

Fortunately the wife of the Director-general called me and asked me to join them for dinner. I will never forget this because their request came when I desperately needed it. My God had not forgotten me help came from unexpected quarters.

I had send change-of-address cards and some people returned a friendly message, as is customary. But once I had finished unpacking I went through the messages again and whilst looking at them one in particular caught my attention.

A good friend had sent the card. She was a beautiful, married woman with a baby girl. Something peculiar struck me because she wrote that she had something to tell me and she had signed the message with her name only. I felt a bit worried so I called her to invite her out to dinner.

On entering the restaurant I could not believe my eyes. There was nothing left of this once beautiful woman. She was all skin and bones and the spark she used to have in her eyes had disappeared completely. She told me she had married too young and that she was very unhappy with her husband. She was also afraid of her parents and did not know which way to turn. I felt she had crossed my path for a reason.

First of all I tried to ascertain whether it was possible for them to get back together again. I knew her husband and perhaps it was worth a try but it soon became abundantly clear there was no way they would ever be reconciled. I decided to help and support her, also because I could not bear the idea of her lovely little girl having to suffer. So she left her husband and moved back in with her parents until a rental house would be available for her. Once that had been accomplished I helped her furnish the house and when she moved in with her daughter the spark in her eyes returned.

We used to meet occasionally and one evening she asked me to accompany her to a 'reading'. This was something spiritual, as far as I could gather, which would involve having my 'flower', 'stem', 'roots' and 'charkas' read. If they would find any obstructions they would tell me. Well, all this was for the open sandals woolly socks types as far as I was concerned but I let her talk me into it.

At the Centre for Life and Intuition three men sat down in front of me and told me through metaphors what they saw. I was sceptic at first but when they told me that I had had a serious problem with my parents at the age of 21, I was hooked. How could they possibly know about that? I was wide awake now and listened to them telling me the story of my life. All I had to do was to say my name every once and a while. It was impressive, to say the least, and I learned a lot about myself. Of course I did possess a certain amount of self-knowledge but it was quite something else listening to complete strangers telling you who you are.

The friend, in the meantime, had started taking spirituality classes and they taught her, amongst other things, to train others in developing their intuition and feeling. She told me most people attending these classes were having troubled relationships and had problems dealing with their feelings. As part of these classes she had to go to a castle in the middle of nowhere to take an exam and she asked whether I could join her and look after her daughter. I decided to help her once more because she had no one else she could ask.

Gradually I had gotten to know her better and I sometimes called her Mrs IQ and sometimes Mrs EQ. She had never been able to strike a balance between down-to-earth pragmatic matters and her feelings. Her parents had owned a shop and had had no time to raise her. She was unbalanced which was why she had started taking these classes in the first place.

Once I had arrived at the castle I noticed this Jesus look-alike with long hair and a white suit. He turned out to be the 'teacher'. Over dinner he tried to look me deep into my eyes. I looked back at him without averting my eyes. I did not trust him. I soon concluded that he had indoctrinated all those taking part with his ideas. I sensed something bad was going on there.

I discovered that all the married participants went for a divorce afterwards and had embarked on relationships with fellow participants, which was against the rules. I finally understood what had led to my friend's divorce. All of a sudden they run into people who are in touch with their feelings and it is such a pleasant alternative to the unfeeling relationship at home.

Every morning session started off with a communal chanting session in front of a couple of photographs and a Buda statue. I refused to take part. During the week my friend got involved with a fellow participant. I tried to reason with her but to no avail. She was beyond help.

I spent the entire week walking and playing with my friend's two year-old daughter. We walked together and while walking she discovered the big world out there. I enjoyed her inquisitive nature and many participants were surprised by the fact that I found more pleasure in the company of a two-year old than in attending the sessions. I enjoyed being on this trip of discovery with the child and I felt that being there for her made a difference.

I learned that there is more that we do not know than that we do know. There is a spiritual world around us and I was becoming more convinced of that. I did notice, though, that some people try to abuse other people's weaknesses. I do not take to that well.

It's all sales

Sometimes it seems easier to make a deal with people who are weaker than we are. But be careful! Sometimes it is easy to push people into placing an order. However, if the customer is not convinced of the merits of your product and is left with the feeling of being talked into it, this might backfire. Your product or service might be good but if the customer is not familiar with all its merits he will not experience the merits of the product and will perhaps even do business with a competitor. The sales process needs to be followed through with every single customer. If that happens, you make a deal that will stick.

A bad sales woman

She came from a different country with a different culture and worked in my department at the computer centre. She lived on her own but was well able to deal with all her male colleagues. She was kind and smiled often.

One day something terrible happened to her. On her way from work to home she was mugged in the park. Her purse was stolen and during the attack she badly injured her knee. With her mobile phone she managed to contact a colleague who rushed to her side and called 911. At the hospital they operated on her knee immediately but she would never be able to do sports again and had a long recovery period ahead of her.

For her colleagues this was unsettling news and we tried to do whatever we could to make things easier for her. Our HR Manager was a sociable person and made sure that the physical side of her recovery was taken care of. He made all the arrangements for her recovery period for her and left nothing to chance.

After about six months she returned to work part time. She was very emotional but her colleagues tried to understand what she had been through and sympathised with her. She received lots of attention and she obviously enjoyed it. She did cry a lot, though.

When she went back to work full-time she was in the habit of crying at the slightest excuse. Whenever a colleague asked her to do something she did not like she would start to cry. I noticed that her colleagues had started to avoid her and that she did not earn her salary. In the end it came down to emotional blackmail.

I discussed my observations with the HR Manager and her supervisor, the Head of the Computer Centre. The HR Manager suggested therapy and the Head of the Computer Centre was apprehensive about the consequences if he was to tell her the truth. There was nothing for it but talking to her myself. The others warned me in advance about the possible consequences.

The night before I was to talk to her I was wide-awake, I meditated and prayed to my God. This was about a human being and what would happen if I approached her in the wrong way? My God gave me peace and I finally fell asleep knowing what I had to do.

The next day I asked my secretary to invite her to come in for coffee. She accepted of course and she was pleased that the Director wanted to have a word with her. I was very friendly towards her and expressed once more my sympathy regarding the horrible accident.

I asked her whether she thought the company had supported her sufficiently and she answered that the company had done so. She started crying again but I ignored that and continued talking to her about her behaviour and the emotional blackmail she was using to have her way with her colleagues. She was visibly shocked by my words and stopped crying immediately. I finally asked her whether she really wanted to have her life ruined by one single incident, no matter how bad the incident had been.

I asked her to think about what I had just said but I noticed that I had hit close to home. I had opened her eyes by simply confronting her with her behaviour. She came back to the office to do her job and slowly but surely she once more enjoyed the work and the smile came back.

I learned that after an incident or accident some people no longer live in the real world. They are afraid of confrontation, but the confrontation does need to take place at definitely at the right time and by the right person.

It's all sales

Also in sales it can take a while before the customer has reached a decision. The customer is well informed; all arguments are met, and still no decision. Sometimes it helps to push the customer in the right direction by simply asking why nothing has been decided yet. This will lead to additional information that would otherwise have remained hidden. Many salespeople are apprehensive of taking this step because they are afraid they might lose the order. But please give this approach a try, you will find that it actually works.

Dealing with General Management

Pressure was mounting for the Management of our company to introduce new products in order to counteract the threat of the introduction of the single currency (Euro). A large part of the lucrative exchange of European foreign currency would stop overnight with the launch of the Euro and our border exchange offices were facing difficult times. Expanding business to the borders of Europe was a possible option but difficult and time consuming.

Another option was to introduce new products. The touristic and telecom products were not lucrative enough by far. We had to try to and promote the fact that our bank would offer services 24 hours a day seven days a week, also to third parties.

New managers were appointed to solve the problems, but most of them turned out to be unsuitable for the task at hand and many left through the backdoor. The opposition against change within the company was almost insurmountable and the employees were trained to sell the current products. It was not easy to carry through a process of change because company culture and Management did not want to cooperate.

The Director-general and I were good friends. I had learned a lot from him and ever since I had joined the Board of Directors he acted as my coach with regard to the general management of the company. He and his wife, who had also been employed by the company, invited me to dinner at their home on a regular basis, also at weekends. I thoroughly enjoyed those dinners and the brainstorming sessions that accompanied the food. We talked about company strategy and policy and possible new products. I loved introducing new products and I liked modernisation and innovation because of the energy it generated.

I became increasingly involved in the general management of the company. I did have to face the fact that not everybody was pleased with that development. A number of fellow board members were not amused and the Comptroller in particular resented my presence.

It was not always easy for me to deal with these sentiments for I only had one goal; winning for the company and its employees. I loved my company and most of its loyal hard-working employees.

Time was against us; pressure was mounting which led to an increasing battle at the top. The top job was at stake now; who was to succeed the Director-general. This battle was more important to some than the new products and services. Power was the name of their game.

I learned that not every manager works only for the good of the company. Own interests prevail on most occasions. It is always for the best for a company if the interest of the individual is the same as that of the company and if that is the case, 1 + 1 will make 3.

In principle everybody is always looking after his own interests. It is the general principle of self-preservation. Yet, if everybody would act selfishly all the time there would be no society left. People are different because of their own personal qualities and therefore will choose their own individual approach. What is the most effective way to reach your goal? It is a combination of you as a person and your surroundings. A salesperson who feels a bond with the company he works for, is much more capable of offering products to his customers than someone who is just doing his job. That is the added value.

Not selling to women

For my secretaries these were amusing times. They sensed interesting movements from all sorts of women who were circling me. Sometimes they told me it would be good for me to allow a woman into my life again but I was not ready. I was hurt and I wanted to take ample time to determine what I had done wrong in my previous relationship. I wanted to learn from my mistakes and not make the same ones again.

What *did* bother me was that those around me treated me differently. In the past I could take women out to dinner and now I was no longer able to do so anymore. It was not as if the women were not interested anymore, their partners were the ones who objected. As far as they were concerned I was competition. I was single and a company Director, which put me in a league of my own. I felt bad about it for I had not changed but my surroundings had. I just had to come to terms with it.

And there was also the matter of my principles. In the past I had witnessed on many occasions the problems that secret relationships at work can bring about. In particular if one of those involved was attached, it could lead to complicated situations. I had decided never to get involved with someone at work and now that I was single I still stuck to my decision. It made it easy for me to deal with the woman at work. They felt I did not pose a threat and that they could talk to me openly and honestly. I stuck to my principle and it served me well.

Unfortunately my principles did not deter some of my female colleagues. Some were very interested in the 'single director' and he became a very desirable object. My secretaries were having a wonderful time for they had front row seats. They were onto the women before I even noticed what was going on. Sometimes my secretary would inform me tactfully.

During a new year's reception as soon as the dancing had started I saw the female HR executive heading straight towards me wearing this enormous hat. She wanted to ask me to dance but I was absolutely not interested and I went for the gents' room straight away. I did not return until most of those present were already on the dance floor with a partner.

There was also the secretary of a fellow director. She kind and had an awful lot to talk about with my secretaries and stopped by on a regular basis. If I came in later, I was greeted by meaningful looks from my secretaries. I tried to avoid her in order not to give her false hope.

And there was also the friendly coffee lady who would turn bright red whenever she came into my office. She was very nice and once gave me the business card of a physiotherapist /haptonomist. Later in life I would be grateful for the address she gave me.

My secretary felt she could not leave me to my own devices and had, without me knowing, contacted a dating agency and had given them my name and phone number. On a Sunday afternoon (the most lonely time of the week for a bachelor) they called me. Someone from the agency asked whether they could start looking (at a charge) for a suitable partner. I turned down their services because I was not ready to allow a woman into my wife.

The next day I was greeted by the meaningful looks of my secretary who asked after my weekend. I told her what had happened and we laughed about it. She just wanted me to be happy again. She meant well.

I learned that there are people who really care about you and your happiness. But I could and would not harm women needlessly and that is not always an easy thing to do because love makes blind.

It's all sales

As a salesperson it is never in your best interest to circumvent the issue. When customers make a proposition you cannot live up to, you might consider leaving the matter open instead of stating clearly both the limitations of the product as well as the advantages. Later on in the sales process this may back fire. With an ambiguous answer the customer might think that your answer is affirmative. When it leads to an order, the customer will notice that you do not meet expectations and may change his mind.

No sale without intuition

One day during an indoor soccer match I got injured. It was not the first time during my long soccer career but I felt that this time it was different. It was painful and I knew this time it could not be cured by rest alone. I had to go to a physiotherapist. I looked for the card the nice coffee lady had given me and dialled the number on the business card. I made an appointment for the next day.

I had not given any thought to the fact that this therapist was also a haptonomist. During my first visit she let me into the secret of haptonomy. What it came down to is that the balance between body and mind can be restored through massage and conversation.

She discovered that the injury to my leg was caused by back problems and she asked me to tell her about my life. I told her about my divorce and my work whilst she was touching some parts of my body. She discovered that I did not respond in any way and determined that I had closed myself off from my feelings and intuition because of all the misery I had been through.

I went to visit her every week and slowly but surely she restored my feeling and intuition. I learned many valuable lessons in life from her and after she massaged my stomach I would end up crying later that evening because that is where my feelings were located. She held my hand and I felt the energy coming back to me.

Her treatment changed me in a natural and positive way. I did feel a bit unstable because all certainties I had had in life fell away and I had to reconstruct them on the basis of not just rationality but also with feeling and intuition.

She also helped me to learn to receive instead of giving all the time. She told me people have an inner circle and an outer circle. The inner circle comprises people you think care about you. In the outer circle you will find your acquaintances. She asked me (because she knew I always took the initiative) not to send the people in my inner circle a card for Christmas nor call them. I just had to wait and see what would happen. I was shocked by the result because it was the loneliest Christmas I had in my entire life. I was very sad, alone and lonely that Christmas but it was undoubtedly an eye opener.

Another lesson she taught me was to learn to look at people who had treated me badly in life and who had hurt me. I thought about these people and I discovered that they were not doing well (cerebral infarction, lost a child, cancer etc.) It shocked me because although they had hurt me this was not what I wanted. It became clear to me that I was a rich man because I was in good health and able to do a job I liked.

Now I could start to learn to enjoy life and my freedom. I lived without hating these people but I was convinced that you could not treat others badly without being punished for this. It was not up to me to pass judgement. Evil brings its own punishment.

Haptonomy changed my life and I was once more enjoying life and using my common sense and intuition. It made my job as a director and manager a lot easier.

These lessons would remain important to me for the rest of my life. I felt fit and in balance and 'rich'. I thanked my God for all these riches.

It's all sales

The above is a genuine lesson of life. Hanging on to all the bad things that happen to us in our lifetime will lead nowhere. Look at the things you have and what you can achieve and how many people you can gather around you. The world is much bigger than the circle you have drawn around you. Every day offers new opportunities to meet fun, interesting and kind people. The only thing you have to do yourself is live.

A shareholder not interested in selling

The struggle for power became fiercer. Our major shareholder was no longer satisfied with the continuance of the process of introducing new services. The shareholder comprised a conglomerate of financial subsidiaries and was not pleased with our attempts to expand our banking products and in doing so competing with other banks that were part of the concern.

The shareholder had already let us know what they were up to for they had blocked two initiatives with special companies that had been interested in banking transactions for their customers and members through our company.

The shareholder assigned a new deputy to our company who was to discourage our banking initiatives and to reduce our banking activities. This new director had been working for the major shareholder for a long time and the concern management knew they could trust him to look after their interests. In addition he also landed the position of manager of a professional soccer team, sponsored by our shareholder. He was preoccupied with this new job.

One of the first things he established was to separate the banking figures from those of the other parts of our company aiming at obtaining an overview of the revenue of both separate parts of the company. His aim was to put a stop to all banking activities and his behaviour was outright negative towards new banking initiatives generated by our Management. There were a few within the company who supported the new director because they had something to gain. For his cunning plans the new director used a young financial employee (econometrist) I had appointed myself. This youngster had a mind of his own and revelled in conjuring up figures and not think about what his figures could mean to the future of his company. His behaviour annoyed me no end and I tried to point out other financial aspects to him. Unfortunately I failed in doing so, his figures were all he cared about.

It finally dawned upon me that this would inevitably lead to the end of my company. The major shareholder and management did not see eye to eye with regard to the future of the company. And unfortunately none of the new products were as lucrative as the current products. After the introduction of the single currency (Euro) we would have to close down some of our heavily guarded and therefore expensive branch offices (especially those close to the border).

The lesson I learned from this was that the interests of the shareholders can differ from those of company management. The shareholder always wins the battle.

Also in sales the interests of management can differ from those of the salesperson. Management should look ahead and take strategic decisions. Sales of a popular product can decrease in the near future because of market developments. Before that happens management should look ahead and introduce new products. The turnover of new products is not worth mentioning. If you were to rely for the full 100% on your old product you would still make a profit and therefore at that point in time take more provision. Yet in the long run problems will arise ...

No gentlemen's agreement

After my divorce I had helped my ex-wife to find an apartment. She had been able to buy a suitable furnished apartment and I had applied on her behalf for a mortgage with our company. As far as I was concerned it was a regular mortgage application.

One of my colleagues seemed determined to deal with the application personally and asked me to come round to his office to discuss the mortgage. He approached the whole matter rather seriously and insisted that he wanted to help me secure an advantageous mortgage.

I had never asked him to do this, for I never meant to be an exception to the rule. If he felt he had to be nice to me it was his decision and I was not going to dissuade him. I regarded it as a gentlemen's agreement, something that is never discussed. Gentlemen's agreements are agreements in a social network that are never mentioned.

Two years later when the power struggle for the top job was at its peak the same colleague came to pay me a visit. His aim was to join the Board of Directors and he asked me to put in a good word for him. I told him I had no influence whatsoever on who was to be promoted to that position but he insisted that I should support his candidacy and talk to the Director-general.

I tried to divert his attention but then he got angry with me and reminded me of the time he had done me a favour with the mortgage application for my ex-wife. I only looked at him and asked him to change the conditions of my ex-wife's mortgage into the standard conditions straight away. He was obviously not a real gentleman.

I learned that when some people are under a lot of pressure they go to great lengths to reach their goal. The conveniently ignore a gentlemen's agreement.

It is well possible that the sales process is successful and the customer still turns down the proposal for no apparent reason. As a salesperson you usually try to determine what you did wrong. Instead, try to put into perspective what happens at the customer's of the deal. Could it be possible that the CEO of your contact is on friendly terms with a competitor? Now all of a sudden your contact needs to deal with a competitor. Do you think he savours the fact that he is sent on an errand by his boss? Do you think he would inform you if that was the case or would he give you a false reason? If you do not see through these proceedings you will draw the wrong conclusions.

Having to deal with love stories

My mother had been admitted to hospital unexpectedly. She was in pain and it was decided to remove her spleen. Fortunately the operation was successful and my mother made a speedy recovery. My father now had to look after himself but he also insisted on visiting his wife at the hospital twice a day. He would visit her during the afternoon visiting hours, stay at the hospital while having his sandwich and visit her once more during the evening visiting hours.

One day I had decided to take the afternoon off to join my father at the hospital. I had planned on taking him to a restaurant, have dinner and get back in time for the evening visiting hours. My father liked the idea and together we had dinner. During dinner he constantly consulted his watch for he did not want to be late for visiting hours.

Back at the hospital, while we were waiting for the doors to the ward to open, I received a business phone call. When the doors opened my father was the first one to enter the ward and on he went to visit his wife. I decided to deal with the phone call first and when I had finished I looked around me until my eyes fixed on a beautiful image. It was my parents walking hand in hand through the hospital corridor. They had been married for sixty years and they were still together, sharing. Suddenly I felt what I was missing, somebody who loves you unconditionally.

Around the same time one Sunday night one of my employees called me. She told me that her manager sent her love e-mails and text messages and that he consistently tried to phone her. I could not understand the manager's behaviour, he seemed to have been happily married. Apparently he had fallen in love.

I advised her to make it clear to him that she was not interested. If that would not do the trick, I would talk to him myself. She took my advice and it stopped right there and then. Because of these love stories I realised how lonely and alone I was. I devoted a lot of energy to my work but in the end it did not offer enough satisfaction.

Before I knew what happened I found myself sitting behind my PC browsing the Internet, looking for a dating site. On one of these sites I got in touch with a woman who was divorced like me and we started e mailing. It was not easy to put the story of my divorce into words and the exercise made me understand why psychiatrists sometimes have people write down their problems.

Writing about your experiences helps to come to terms with them. We served as each other's psychiatrist when we told each other our life stories. We were very different, though, and we never met in person. When she got involved with a new partner I missed her daily e-mails.

This lesson was about the process of healing after getting hurt. My period of recovery was slow and such a process covers a different time span for everyone. There is nothing else for it but to stay your course.

Also in sales you have to deal with setbacks, perhaps even more than in matters of the heart. And this makes sense because in sales, and in acquisition in particular, meeting new people is an important part of the job. Every attempt we make could turn into failure. When it comes to acquisition it is not easy to make an appointment. One indicator: one out of ten cold calls will lead to an appointment. That means you will get 'no' for an answer nine out of ten times. Nine times someone will let you know that no matter how good you think your product is, they are not interested. Remaining confident in your own success is difficult in cases like that.

Dealing with the secretaries

Since my appointment to the position of Director I was responsible for a department comprising about 100 people. This meant that I had to work even more hours than I already did. I lived alone and therefore had the opportunity to spend most of my time on my work. I started work every day at 7.30 a.m. by going through the mail and reading my e-mails and preparing for the day to come. Meetings usually started at nine.

Having eight meetings a day was not uncommon and in order to keep abreast of things I had to read the briefing documents at home the night before. Some strategic memos I wrote myself, usually on Sunday mornings. The briefing documents for the Board of Director's Meeting would usually be distributed on the Friday afternoon preceding the Board Meeting on Monday. I had an average working week of 60 hours, but I enjoyed the work.

I was in the habit of chairing meetings and usually my secretary would take minutes. I was well organised and my meetings went according to schedule. My secretary therefore enjoyed taking minutes, especially because I whenever we reached a decision I would summarise the main points.

She would type up the minutes in concept first and I would correct them if necessary before distributing them. For some of the meetings I did not chair but just took part in, they would usually ask my secretary to take minutes as well. This was to my advantage because it enabled me to steer things in the right direction through the minutes.

One of my fellow managers usually made a mess of his meetings. He was the chairperson but kept elaborating upon his own action points without solving a single one of them. We only had one hour for these meetings and after about half hour I would usually gradually take over without him noticing so we could still finish on time.

During one of those meetings things were not moving fast enough according to my secretary. She yawned quite loudly and from her body language it became clear that she had had enough. She kicked me from under the table and said 'take charge…. take charge, now!' It made me laugh and I did take charge of proceedings. My colleague must have noticed this time but he did not respond. Apparently he did not mind.

Another fellow manager always spend the first half hour of his meetings giving vent to his frustrations about the Comptroller, the Director-general and other colleagues. It always turned into a one-man show. My secretary did not want to take minutes during these meeting, fortunately his own secretary was quite proficient at taking minutes.

The lesson I learned was that it pays off to perform as team with your secretaries. You do something for them and they do a lot in return. Working together as equals is the most effective and efficient form of cooperation. I enjoyed working together with the secretaries devoted a lot of effort to cooperating with them successfully.

Selling after resigning

In the meantime my daughter had graduated from the School for Business Administration and Economics and had secured her first job with a financial establishment. I asked her what her goals were and she told me that she wanted to do the same things I did. I had the idea that she only saw the positive aspects of my job but that did not matter at the time. She was highly motivated but at the same time managed to negotiate a 36-hour working week. This surprised me but as my daughter pointed out she did not want to become as crazy about work as I was. Well, I had to accept this.

Still, she had trouble finding her feet in a day job. She complained about missing the freedom of her student days. She did not like having to stick to all the rules and procedures stipulated by her employer. She complained about it often and I got the feeling that having a day job somehow hurt her.

One day she phoned because she was angry with her manager for reprimanding her. It had been a beautiful sunny day and she had been out to lunch with a colleague and had forgotten all about the time. She did not understand the attitude of her manager. This had been the first really warm summer's day why could he not understand that? I listened to her story but did not respond directly, I just laughed. Her manager was actually helping me and I felt pleased about it.

After two years my daughter wanted to change jobs and found a new challenge. She resigned and was subject to two months notice. One night she called me again. She was clearly upset and wanted to talk to me. Of course I wanted to talk to her and I told her I would see her after work.

As soon as she entered my apartment she burst out and said that her manager had brought her to account on the fact that according to her contract she had to work 36 hours a week. My daughter did not understand why he was picking on her. She had already resigned and he still forced her to work all these hours. She did not understand and had come to me for support.

I made her a cup of tea first to calm her down and in my mind I knew that I had to approach her tactfully. The last thing I wanted was to upset my daughter even more. So I asked her quietly whether the company still paid her a full salary every month. She answered with an affirmative. I saw this spark in her eye and I could tell she knew where I was heading. I advised her to work the assigned hours and to apologise to the manager. At the end of the day he was responsible for writing her reference letter. My daughter calmed down and took my advice.

I learned that it is not easy to coach your daughter in an honest and sincere manner. But in the end it is always for the best. We remained good friends for life.

It's all sales

What it comes down to, is that we have to sell ourselves to everyone. And not only to those we think we might need later on in life. Be sure to show certain aspects of yourself not directly related to sales. It is about you as a person. If you are able to make yourself accessible you will notice that people will be drawn to you. What could be more profitable in sales?

A small company is not important

At the beginning of the year our hardware supplier once more assigned a new Account Manager to my company. An appointment was made and once again his predecessor did not accompany the new Account Manager.

I decided to play the same game I had been playing over the past years to see if they had learned their lesson. And also this Account Manager started off by asking what my company was all about and informed after our products. I looked him in the eye and I also asked him politely to contact his predecessor since I had no intention telling the same story every year.

This Account Manager got incredibly angry and informed me, while finishing his coffee, that he regretted coming out here because my company did not feature on his list of ten most important companies. As far as he was concerned our company did not matter at all.

I told him to leave my office immediately. I phoned his manager and informed him that I did not want to meet this Account Manager ever again. This is exactly what happened and I was assigned an Account Manager who had done his 'homework'.

As far as I am concerned, in sales customer is always king! Despite this bad Account Manager I kept buying their product, though.

It's all sales

A salesperson that communicates in the way described will not last long in the job. The question that arises is in what way are customers discussed within the company? Can you hold it against a salesperson if within the company customers are discussed in a discriminatory fashion? Make sure that it is part of your company culture that everybody is aware of the fact if it was not for the customer, the company would not exist.

Selling transaction terminals

The successful cooperation on the introduction of electronic payment with the major Telecom Operator had led to the decision to continue working together on new and innovative products, using the combined infrastructure.

This major Telecom Operator was, of course, also interested in establishing its own bank or acquiring a bank. They sold their products and services to almost every household in the Netherlands and as is common practice for every large enterprise they were actively looking in the market for suitable banking products. The difference was, though, that this Telecom Operator would examine first whether cooperation with a large bank was feasible. If that was not an option they would consider acquiring a smaller bank.

As an extra service we had developed a very attractive information terminal that resembled a normal phone booth but it served to make and pay for last-minute hotel reservations. For this purpose we had reached an agreement with a chain of hotels. They would inform us on their vacancies and room rates by means of a PC linked to our central system.

Any traveller looking for a hotel room could select one, make a reservation and pay by credit card. We had discovered that many tourists (and in particular those travelling by train) came to the Netherlands without making any arrangements. Especially young back packers on a trip around the world wanted to spend the night in a hotel room every now and then to have a decent night's sleep instead of sleeping in the park or at the train station.

We already had visions of having this product available on the Internet but at that point in time secure payment on the Internet was not possible. We had to be patient but we knew our infrastructure could deal with these transactions.

On a personal level I thoroughly enjoyed working on innovative projects and I was always personally involved. The major Telecom Operator must have thought I made my mark as a project manager because that continued to be my position in every joint enterprise.

It made me strong and I was capable of reaching quite a few goals within their organisation probably because sometimes it takes a new pair of eyes to put things into proper perspective.

I learned that when it came to motivation and enthusiasm new developments always did it for me. I always learned something from it and I enjoyed being innovative.

It does not work this way for everyone but most salespeople want to come up with a new story. What becomes apparent is that salespeople have the tendency to add something new to their sales pitch. This seems to be happening to add some variety to their story. Subconsciously they think they have already told the full story to the customer. Because of this the message might level off and as a result may overshoot the mark and lead to a negative outcome.

Selling through a dating site

Since I was too old to go clubbing and meet people in that way a dating site on the Internet seemed like a good alternative. I soon found that the free-of-charge dating sites were useless because many of the women were in it for the money. The people on those sites were not serious and you could never be quite sure whom you were dealing with. Hence my decision to register with a paid dating site.

At first it was an exciting and fun way to meet women. I thought and felt I had learned my lessons from the past and was ready to embark on a new relationship. I had been single for four years now and since my daughter had left home it was very quiet around the house. My feelings were a bit ambiguous though; on the one hand I enjoyed coming home without any fuss. And sometimes I came home and I felt lonely and missed having somebody fuss over me.

Financially I could only get involved with a woman if she were financially independent. The alimony I had to pay to my ex-wife and the costs of putting my daughter through college were still too high. By now I was used to my freedom and was therefore only interested in a LAT relationship. Living together was as far as I was concerned no longer an option. Mind you, all these decisions were taken by the head and not the heart. And, for that matter, I was a healthy man and I wanted to have sex with a woman again.

Another reason why I was interested in a relationship was that I noticed that at work I was chasing women. I hated myself because I had always wanted to keep business and private separate and that was still what I wanted but I could not help it. My male hormones were playing up.

It was easier said than done to get in touch with women through a dating site. Usually the people frequenting these sites were much younger and particularly women of my age were far and few between. And I also noticed that most women were after spiritual men who were in touch with their own feelings.

That had obviously been a major frustration with most women in their previous relationship. Well, what is a man supposed to do to get in touch with women? I lowered my age on the site (a downright lie, but I looked younger anyway) and added the word 'spiritual' to my profile. That is how I met this beautiful Chinese lady.

This first relationship was solely based on sex. Both of us had not had sex for a number of years and we obviously had some catching up to do. I felt ashamed when I read a book about divorces and had to conclude I was doing exactly what every divorced man does. It was nothing out of the ordinary. This was what we both wanted and we discussed the matter openly with each other. I told her that as soon as she met another man I would disappear from her life altogether.

It had nothing to do with true love it was all about sex. I had given her a beautiful dress on a Saturday to wear for a Christmas dinner party with friends. That night she started a relationship with one of the friends.

Later that week she phoned me and she cried while she apologised. She felt terrible because she knew that I was a decent man. She did not understand her own behaviour. I comforted her but I felt hurt and betrayed at the same time. We are still friends, though, and she is still in a relationship with that same friend. It all turned out for the best.

There were also contacts that made it all worthwhile. It was fun and exciting to receive an e-mail from someone and answering it. I was also able to help a foreign woman who needed emergency surgery. She could not afford it and I was able to help her. She was very grateful and since she owned her parent's home she arranged for me to get my money back as soon as she would be able to sell the house. In the mean time she is still paying me back in monthly instalments. There are indeed honest people on dating sites.

I learned that sex without love was not what made me happy. I cherished the experience, though and it did wonders for my ego. It was good to know I still counted for something as a lover.

It's all sales

From a sales point of view: Sex without love is big business. What we often encounter in sales is that the customer switches supplier without informing you. This behaviour stems from a lack of personal involvement with the customer. That is, if the product and or service is still satisfactory. Sometimes a customer relationship is so strong that a customer does not dare to tell you about the switch. He is afraid you will be disappointed. Conclusion: as a salesperson you always have to be on guard and able to interpret signals properly.

Selling fraud

The General and Technical Services Department was now part of my division and my goal was to make the processes in this department more effective and efficient to increase costs effectiveness. Management had agreed with my plans.

Different projects were initiated and one of the projects aimed at process streamlining within the Purchasing Department. The Head of the Purchasing Department had been with the company for many years and had had to report to many of my fellow directors like the Sales and Marketing Director and the Comptroller at one time or another. He seemed a kind man and was popular with his colleagues.

In his private life he was a huge Formula One racing fan and sometimes he would take some of his colleagues to watch a race. It struck them that he was well-connected there and always received VIP treatment. According to rumours he had married into wealth and did not have to work for a living.

When I objectively assessed his work as a buyer I was not impressed. He drove a company lease car and was usually on the road visiting our suppliers. As far as I was concerned that was the wrong approach for who was the one buying and who was selling? I talked to him about my plans regarding the department and compiled a project plan to initiate the improvements. I appointed him Project Manager.

He seemed to agree with my plans since he had no choice but nothing happened. He was of course too busy and so he was assigned an organisation information analyst who was to carry out the work for him. A fellow director, who had been his superior in the past, paid me a visit and told me to treat the Head of Purchasing with respect and not put too much pressure on him. The way he looked at it the Head of Purchasing was very important to our company.

On any busy day people used to queue in front of one of our 80 branch offices to carry out their transactions. A speedy transaction at the service desk was therefore of the utmost importance. An important part of the process was of course the receipt. It was essential that there were always sufficient printer rolls available to print the receipts. No printer rolls meant no transactions and not being able to serve customers.

Everyone at the branch offices and the main office was aware of the importance of the supply of printer rolls. Whenever the Head of Purchasing needed a signature to order printer rolls and had to arrange for a rush payment, all managers cooperated. Everybody helped him and trusted him because they were aware of the importance to our company.

138

One day the organisation information analyst came to visit me and he told me that he had discovered that the actual supply of printer rolls did not match the number of printer rolls ordered and paid for. Immediately alarm bells went off inside my head. There was something very wrong here and I notified the Director-general immediately. He in turn brought in the Internal Accountant services to investigate the matter.

The results of the investigation showed that the Head of Purchasing had been involved in fraudulent activities concerning printer roll orders, deliveries and payments for more than a decade. Through a fake company registered to the Head of Purchasing the money was transferred into his own account. It was truly outrageous and many of his colleagues had trusted him and felt betrayed. It turned out that he also had two separate families.

I learned that it is very difficult to trust people when it comes to business matters. Personally I had always believed in keeping private and business matters separate. You always need to be on the alert and remain objective.

It's all sales

Because a salesperson's job mostly involves communication and since he depends heavily on relationships it seems as if he has many 'friends'. It is difficult to distinguish between them. In general business friendships will last as long as the business link still exists. If this link is broken because the salesperson moves into a different line of business it is difficult to remain friends. New friendships will emerge.

Dealing with a gambling addiction

This young man had been employed at the calculus centre of our company for many years. He worked shifts and was always willing to work overtime or help out his colleagues if they wanted to swap shifts. He told me he enjoyed working with us for the alternative was working at his father's Chinese restaurant, something he did not appreciate at all.

He was an ideal employee and was always available. He lived on his own at a walking distance of our main office. His work was his life and his colleagues were his friends since he hardly had a social life. He did not speak Dutch or English well, which often led to funny misunderstandings between him and his colleagues.

One day the banking director, my colleague, came round to my office and told me that the Chinese man had applied for a personal loan. The banking director had talked to him personally but had some doubts on why he needed the loan. He asked me to make some inquiries.

This was a private matter and I knew I had to tread carefully, so I used my social network in the department to dig up some more background information. It was not hard to find out what the problem was because the Chinese man had tried to borrow money from his colleagues on a number of occasions. It turned out that he frequently went to the casino in town and had ended up having serious gambling debts. His creditors and gambling friends now demanded their money back.

I knew what I had to do and I informed his manager that I would have a word with him. I knew the Chinese man respected me and when he entered my room I could feel he was quite nervous. I decided to be strict with him because I sensed this was the best approach for him. A serious in-depth conversation was out of the question because of his limited command of the Dutch language but I did not let that impede the message I wanted to get across. I appreciated this man a lot and owed it to him to play my part well.

He seemed relieved at the opportunity to tell his story. He was in the habit of going to the casino several times a week and had ran up serious debts. He was experiencing severe financial problems and desperately needed the loan. I pretended to be very angry with him and forbade him to ever set foot in a casino again, otherwise he would be fired immediately. He also made him hand in a list of all his creditors and the amounts of money he owed them.

I felt sorry for him. He was so shocked that he even started drooling. I did promise him that if he did what I asked I would help him with his loan application. That is what happened. I made sure the incident was not included in his personnel file. He never went to the casino again and never missed a payment on his loan.

I could not check up on him personally but I relied on my network to inform me if he ran into trouble again. Later on in life I would meet him again on several occasions. He was studying hard, had a job he liked and was doing well.

I learned that it is important to strike the right note with employees. In order to reach your goal it is important to be able to play different parts. I helped a gambler by gambling on the right way to approach him. I owed a lot to my drama lessons.

It's all sales

In sales it happens often that before you get an order you have to invest in a new customer. Sometimes you have to take a customer out to dinner after a sales conversation, or do something to solve one of his problems. These are investments. And investments are expenses because nothing gained nothing ventured. Yet, you never know whether you are actually going to get a return on investment. Is this gambling or daring to stick your neck out?

Bad selling of a case of fraud

The management of our company was caught up in a fight with the major shareholder to preserve the banking activities of our company. These were uneasy times for most of us. The director that was assigned by the major shareholder to reduce our banking activities seized the opportunity to bring in external auditors to investigate the fraud case.

The atmosphere within the company was unpleasant because everybody was busy trying to cover their tracks for nobody wanted to be involved with the Head of Purchasing and this fraud case. Most were afraid because they were not sure whether they could stay clear of suspicion especially now that external auditors were involved. Only our legal advisor enjoyed the situation as only he could enjoy someone else's misery. That was common knowledge.

I was convinced this fraud case would leave me unscathed. Given my past experience at another bank with the tax inspectors of the Inland Revenue I had flatly refused to sign any orders and payments I did not know anything about. I did hold the firm's procuration but I never used it. I had learned my lesson.

I told the external auditors that we had discovered the fraud because we had instigated the process of reorganising the General and Technical Services Department. I stayed clear from internal speculation, arguments and insinuations regarding the fraud case. What did surprise me was that the external auditors reported to our Comptroller. It surprised me because I did not think he was in the clear since he had been in charge of internal finance control during the fraud.

The result of the external auditor's investigation was that the fraud had been going on for more than 15 years and that it involved millions. I was summoned into the Director-general's office and he told me about the consequences of the fraud and much to my surprise also told me some of them concerned me.

Since I had been responsible for the Purchasing Department at the time of the fraud they had decided I was no longer to be responsible for the General and Technical Services Department. Since I had been the one who had discovered the fraud I was allowed to stay on as a manager of the other departments in my division and could remain a member of the Board of Directors. I was absolutely dumbfounded. This was a set-up.

It did not take me long to find out who had set me up. He gave himself away when he laughingly remarked that I had ruined my chances of becoming Director-general. It was the Comptroller who was in league with the director appointed by the major shareholder. It was crystal clear to me that our major shareholder did not appreciate my support to the Director-general and his plans to secure the future of our company. I clearly saw what the future held and I decided not to give up without a fight. The company and its employees deserved it.

I learned once more not to underestimate my enemies. You always have to stay on the alert and look after your own interests. Every weakness you show will be embraced by your enemies and used to hit you where it hurts. You can never trust your colleagues because they all have their own interests at heart.

It's all sales

As soon as you start thinking that you have everything under control you should start paying attention. Paying attention to your own development that is. This could be the moment that you start losing out on results and position. If you want to be a successful salesperson and want to do everything to succeed you need to stay on top of things continuously. Keep yourself informed on market developments, competition developments and trade journals, developments in different markets that might be in keeping with your own market. Be eager when it comes to staying informed.

Dealing with self-knowledge

I was not happy with the dates generated by the paid dating sites on the Internet. I had discovered that Internet profiles were usually not very accurate when I met the lady face-to-face. I was very well aware of the fact that dating site profiles were more or less sales pitches, but still. In some cases I went on a blind date and at first sight I was already disappointed and would still have to sit through dinner with her.

And to be honest, I also have to admit that most women I dated were frustrated about their past relationships and on some occasions I advised them to solve their problems first before embarking on a new relationship. No, I had to face the fact that the results of my blind dates were disappointing.

I did learn quite a lot about myself through the conversations with my dates. I also met one lady my own age with two kids. She was financially independent and her son was training to become a pilot and her daughter was in High School. We got along well as friends but I was not in love.

She was very interested in the signs of the Zodiac and it turned out we were both Scorpios. She had spent quite some time studying the star signs and asked me for my place and time of birth. Since I did not know my exact time of birth I had to call my mother to find out.

She promised she would explain my star sign into detail but that it would take some time. After two weeks she phoned me and asked me after a particular month in my life for she was certain something terrible had happened in my life in that month. It was uncanny because the month she referred to was the month I had divorced my wife and I was absolutely sure I had never told her that.

As a result I became increasingly interested in her story. When she told me her life story I was truly impressed and her story also served as a mirror held up to me. Because of the information she gave me I started thinking about myself and it helped me to change.

We are still friends to this very day and still chat occasionally. She is happily married and has two children with her second husband. A friendship for life.

I once again learned more about myself, and that there is much more to find out about yourself. Every experience adds something towards the inevitable outcome that there is more we do not know than that we do know. I fully accepted that.

Many salespeople find assessments or appraisal interviews tedious because they are confronted with a critical approach to their own performance. It is funny in a sense because we rather avoid criticism because it makes us feel bad whereas in actual fact we can learn something about ourselves. With hindsight we are able to admit that it was worthwhile but at short term we want to avoid it. Our body and mind protect us from bad feelings. Only if the final outcome motivates us we will allow negative feelings.

Bad selling strategy from a Comptroller

The two company directors did not see eye to eye when it came to determining a strategy to secure the company's future. In addition to that, they also clearly disliked each other, which put almost a complete stop to the decision-making process. The atmosphere was downright bad since all managers were fighting for their own survival and were no longer concerned with the company and its future.

Our Comptroller, who had never been a friend to me, thought his time had come to aim for the position of Director-general. Without informing both directors beforehand he contacted the Chairman of the Supervisory Board and told him that both directors were making 'a mess of things' and that the current problems could be solved if they would appoint him Director-general.

The chairman also happened to work for one of our smaller shareholder and in turn informed his fellow supervisors with the major shareholder. From then on events followed each other in rapid succession. The Director-general was relieved from all his responsibilities and sent home. The Director appointed by the major shareholder was assigned to a new position at their head office. A new Director-general was appointed (a friend of one of the supervisors) who was assigned to downsize the company (i.e. cease all banking activities) and restructure the company and prepare for selling-off once the EURO had been introduced.

A horrible situation and I had not been able to do a single thing about it. The major shareholder did not appreciate my support for the fired Director-general, but I never regretted it because from my point of view banking with 24-hour access was our key to securing the future of our company. I was convinced of that.

The good times were gone and I decided to wait taking any decisions regarding my own future because I wanted to do whatever possible to avoid negative consequences for my staff. Somebody was still laughing, though. It was the Comptroller.

The new Director-general started off energetically and left us in no doubt as to his plans. And one of his first actions was to fire the Comptroller on the spot. In his stead he appointed a friend because he did not appreciate people he could not trust and went to talk to supervisors behind his back.

I remembered looking outside the moment the Comptroller left the building, carrying two heavy briefcases. He had never been a friend to me but I could find no joy in his dismissal. At the end of the day he had been dedicated to the company. A sense of sadness engulfed me and I was worried about my own and my staff's future.

I learned that you can only play a game, like the one the Comptroller played, if you know that you are going to win. You always need to take into account that if you lose in a game like this the consequences are severe.

It's all sales

When are risks acceptable? Certainly not when this means that you could lose your job or generate heavy losses. Gambling in sales is unacceptable. This only happens in cases of desperation. In sales it means that if you are unable to assess the implications, research should be carried out. When in doubt start looking for answers, not risks.

Sold by the shareholder

The new Director-general lost no time in showing his hand, for after he had given the Comptroller his marching orders his next move was hardly any better. Because of the fraud case I was no longer responsible for the General and Technical Services Department. My assistant manager had taken over responsibility for that department next to his duties as Chairman of the Works Council. Those employed in this department were not too pleased with this latest decision of the Director-general. They still regarded me as their manager and I was still too taken-up with their wellbeing.

One of the elderly employees in the department was the driver of the company executive car. He had been employed in many different positions and since he was always willing to go the extra mile (day and night) he was well liked. He always made sure that the members of the Board of Directors, including me, would arrive at our destination in time. I only used his services if I were to visit one of the foreign offices.

One day he walked into my office crying like a child for the new Director-general had fired him on the spot. He no longer needed a driver or so he said. From then on everybody was responsible for his or her own transport. I could do nothing but try and comfort the driver and I promised I would help him to negotiate a favourable severance package.

I was downright shocked by the Director-general's action. And it became all the more clear to me what his intentions were. He was to bleed dry this company and take it apart at the same time. In a sense I could understand his motives but I could not understand the way in which he set about dismantling the organisation. How can you treat people badly who have dedicated their lives to the company and who have generated so much profit?

The day after he had fired the driver, the Director-general called him to ask him to drive him in his own car to a business meeting. It was beyond me. How could you do this to someone you have just fired? It was obvious; this Director-general was not capable of empathising with people. It was a warning.

During the next board meeting he unfolded his plans for the future and to me it did not come as a surprise that he was to downsize the company and concentrate only on parts of the company that would prove to be profitable after the introduction of the Euro. All banking activities were to be ceased and existing activities were to be transferred to the bank owned by the major shareholder. There was to be a redundancy scheme for the employees. He would also schedule an appointment with the individual Board Members to discuss with them the personal consequences regarding the changes.

148

Later that week I had my interview and I thought I was prepared for what he was about to tell me. He informed me that given the downsizing of the company a large automation department was no longer required. Therefore I no longer featured in his future plans. I did not say anything; I just looked at him. I tried to look him straight in his cold eyes but he averted them. He was good at talking big but he was not smart. I remained silent and before I left he informed me I was also no longer a member of the Board of Directors. I once again managed to remain silent and left his office.

Inside I was burning with rage and I decided to call a solicitor (I had, after all, taken out insurance for cases like this). We had a lengthy telephone conversation and we agreed it was fortunate that I still had all the appraisals in writing covering all the years I had been employed by the company. His first advice entailed that the Director-general could not dismiss me from the Board of Directors because I had an excellent record of service. This was good news and I and I was well pleased with the support offered by the solicitor. I sent the Director-general an e-mail stating that he could not dismiss me just like that from the Board of Directors.

The support made me feel strong and I decided to stay on for the time being and to fight for the rights of the employees and appropriate redundancy terms. I felt they were at least entitled to that. I was convinced that I could not trust the new Director-general and also, as it turned out, some of my fellow-directors proved to be unreliable.

I learned that after twelve years of hard work it can be made clear to you that it all has been in vain in a mere 15 minutes. That is what it felt like at that moment. Of course all those years have not been in vain because I learned a lot in the process. I had been fighting for this company to overcome the threats posed by the introduction of the Euro, but I had lost. The time had come for me to accept that.

Hard work never guarantees continuity. It does help to improve your position. The problem is that you can assess the situation described above from two different angles. From the employee's point of view "I've been working so hard for all these years and now they drop me just like that". And from management's point of view "We offered him a job for many years and paid him good wages". Every one takes the angle that suits him. In sales it is no different: In the end you use the arguments that suit your needs.

Selling to the enemy

As of now I had a different position within the company. With the support of my solicitor I felt strong and ready to do battle. I was not worried about my own future I just wanted to make sure that the hard-working employees would be treated fairly and with respect by means of a good redundancy terms.

Something did have to happen of course and the company had to downsize in order to survive. I felt responsible for what was happening and I felt I had failed in trying to find profitable alternative products. I understood why it had to happen and I had no problems with the downsizing but I did fear that the new management assisted by the turncoats would not treat the employees properly and fairly.

It was common knowledge that I was in the habit of starting early. As soon as word was out that I opposed the new Director-general, it became rather busy in my office. Many people gathered in there because they were worried about their future and they came to me to find out about decisions made by the Board of Directors.

In return I received much information about the behaviour of the Director-general. He frustrated people endlessly by asking them what they were doing all day long and thereby raising doubts about their dedication. He was highly unpopular and later on I discovered why. He received a bonus paid out of the redundancy fund. If staff decided to leave because they found employment elsewhere, the company would not have to pay them severance pay. This was beneficial to his own bonus.

I was careful not to get in the way of the new Director-general for I did not want to give him reason to fire me. I had obtained my own personnel record from the HR department and had handed it over to my solicitor. Nothing untoward could happen to that. I knew that the Director-general was just waiting for the opportunity to fire me. Which is why I consulted my solicitor every day to discuss every move I intended to make. It worked because the Director-general started to treat me appropriately.

As a member of the Board of Directors I was quite disappointed in the behaviour of my fellow directors. Their behaviour had changed and all of a sudden the HR Director was the Director-general's new best friend. Everything he had arranged with regard to his staff's well being was forgotten and he now came up with the most horrible proposals. He was not responsible for former attainments but the old Board of Directors was.

I took him to task over his behaviour by countermanding every proposal he came up with. I simply reminded him of the arrangements he had made in the past accompanied by a piercing look. He had never had a strong personality and my behaviour forced him into silence. Of course I was able to sustain my remarks with documents written by him from the past. Especially at that time it paid off to be well organised.

I discovered that all the remarks I made during board meetings were not included in the minutes. So I now I made sure I repeated my remarks especially for the secretary to include them in the minutes. The Director-general was not pleased with my actions, but there was nothing he could do about it.

By that time the atmosphere on the work floor was downright bad. Motivation had dropped to an absolute minimum and everyone was on autopilot. No more jokes and laughter. I no longer enjoyed going to work but I felt the time had not yet come to leave. A captain does not abandon a sinking ship.

I learned and understood that in times of trouble there will always be people who will look after their own interests and join the enemy. This for the sake of self-preservation. Personal interests prevail over the interests of the group.

It's all sales

What can you do if in sales things do not work out the way they should. Many salespeople jump at the opportunity to blame others. Salespeople are perfectly able to indicate why a deal was not made. It is much more difficult to determine what you could have done in order to score. You will learn more if you are able to search your own conscience.

Selling your soul for a lease car

The new Director-general could not carry out his downsizing activities without the help and support of certain individuals and consultative bodies. The redundancy terms, for instance, had to be approved by the Works Council. And the Works Council at our company had been elected when the old Board of Directors was still in charge.

Our Works Council mainly consisted of employees from the branch offices and unrest among them was rife. The number of branch offices would be halved because of the introduction of the Euro. Not obtaining the approval from the Works Council would mean an insurmountable obstacle for the new management.

The Chairman of the Works Council had been a good friend of the former Director-general. We had sort of manoeuvred him into that position and had appointed him head of the General and Technical Services Department. He was also known as the company newsletter but was not exactly known for his zest for work.

He still had six months to go before he would retire and was not at all worried about his own future. He had always been in the habit of dropping by at my office to discuss the latest news and gossip. I always thought he of all people would be loyal to the old management because that is what he had always been before.

He drove a company lease car and that pleased him because one of his daughters lived abroad and he would drive out there often at weekends to visit her. Normally this would be rather expensive but because of the lease car it was not.

I noticed that all of a sudden he no longer came to visit me in my office. It seemed as if he was avoiding me. During one of the Board Meetings I found out why. The Director-general had had a word with him and asked him to stay on as Chairman of the Works Council. In exchange he only needed to work for three days a week and was also allowed to keep his lease car. As it turned out, his loyalty was for sale.

I learned that apparently loyalty could be bought and that personal interests will always prevail. I was disappointed in him as a person because he was a religious man and went to church on a regularly.

Salespeople as well as customers are friends as long as it is about business. If a customer decides to switch to another supplier it will always mean that the friendship is over. In other words, in business you do not have friends, just temporary pleasant relationships. In business never rely on friendships but on sales arguments.

Trying to sell giving and taking

The problems at work did not fail to have an effect on me personally. Those were difficult days because once more I had to think carefully about the future. I had to find a job in order to pay my wife's alimony. I still felt responsible to keep my part of the bargain even though I knew she did not live up to her side of the bargain.

I had cancelled my dating site subscription. I was disappointed in the results since the only women I met were those who were interested in me as a provider but were not truly interested in me as a person. My car, house and position were far more important to them. I was disappointed, but I did realise that it was my problem and not theirs.

I felt very lonely at that time. I had spent most of my time working and had acquired many business friends over the years. Yet they were no longer interested, after all, for some of them it was good news that I stood to lose my job. For others like the suppliers it was no longer worth their while for there was no business to be had from me. One man's breath is another man's death. But on the outside I remained the strong man.

Like a true Scorpio I withdrew into my shell. I read a lot about spiritual matters, listened to my favourite music and had started attending haptonomy sessions again. I also relaxed and meditated with my God. I assessed my life and I realised that until then I had had a successful business career but that I had neglected my private life. Where would I go from here? What was it I really wanted?

I had started off working hard in order to provide for my family. Later on I had experienced as a manager what it was like to have power. And now I was left with nothing because I was about to lose my job. Which step was I to take? What was it I wanted from life? What would make me happy?

Once more my God provided me with the answers when I talked to him one night. He told me I had to accept the past and that I should be satisfied with what I had achieved for I was still able to look myself straight in the eye.

I should be proud of the fact that I was 'rich'. Yet, I had to be patient and just take one day at the time, making use of the lessons I had learned from the past. And I had to learn to have faith in whatever the future might bring. Everything was to turn out for the best and I would be able to use my past experiences in the future. These thoughts made me feel more at ease and I could smile again.

These meditation sessions with my God taught me that I had to be myself no matter what. I was a natural giver and did not enjoy receiving I did have to learn somehow how to receive but there was no need to make dramatic changes to my life because the act of giving in itself was enough to make me happy.

I had to continue to believe in my own strength for it had always worked for me in the past. My God returned it to me in an unexpected manner. And when I looked around me there were many people in my life who respected me and loved me. Also the ex-women in my life treated me with respect and wanted me back in their lives. I just had to believe in myself.

I learned that the answers to the real questions will only come when you are experiencing serious problems. Only then will the right answers and insights present themselves. I could always rely on myself.

It's all sales

It is a well-known phenomenon that in the end you will gain more from problems than from successful situations. How often are you able to tell yourself that what happened was for the better, the divorce, this labour dispute, or the argument with a friend. It provides new insights and will clear the air. Why are we then so reluctant to deal with this kind of problems?

A heart of gold does not always sell

This lady had been working for the company for over thirty years. She was employed at the canteen and had watched the company and the number of employees grow considerably. She knew everything there was to know about everybody and wore her heart on her sleeve. If she liked you she would do anything for you, if she did not you had a problem and you were certain to miss out on a cup of coffee.

If you knew her it was obvious to deduct from her body language whether she liked someone or not. For some upstart managers she did not have any respect at all, and one of them was the HR manager. She had given him a piece of her mind once and had told him there and then what she thought of him. Even though the incident took place some years ago it still bothered him and he never lost an opportunity to have her fired.

I liked her a lot and every morning I went to the canteen to get a cup of coffee for one of my secretaries and myself. She was always eager to have a chat and would treat me to one of her dirty jokes and she even liked it better if told her one, something that was audibly appreciated.

She was a simple, straightforward woman with a heart of gold, always going the extra mile. Still, you had to treat her right otherwise she would set her 'man' on you and he was this strong bear-like type who would not hesitate to use his fists in order to protect her interests.

As mentioned earlier, the HR director was still frustrated enough to take on every opportunity to get rid of her. He was pleased as punch when he received a complaint about her making a racist remark to a Jewish employee. He regarded the incident as the perfect opportunity to have her fired. Unfortunately he forgot to mention the fact that she had apologised in writing to the employee and had shown remorse for unintentionally offending him. I had discovered this and confronted the HR manager. He lost again in his quest to fire the canteen lady, which frustrated him even more.

When the new Director-general was appointed he tried again. His behaviour resembled that of a spoiled child and once more he suggested at a Board Meeting to have her fired. However, since a number of external people were employed at the canteen it turned out to be more cost effective to let her stay on and reduce the number of external employees. He once again had to give in and I could not resist smiling at him. He was so pathetic and he did dare to look at me.

Later on, after I had left the company, he tried again. The canteen lady had contacted me to ask whether I would be willing to sign a statement regarding the racist remark and her apologies. I was only too willing to help her and when I gave her the statement she thanked me by presenting me with a lovely bottle of eau de toilette. The HR director wanted to limit her severance pay because of her past behaviour. This sad character lost once more.

I learned that frustrations can drive people crazy and make them do things that are unimaginable. Hate is a bad advisor and it is always better to turn these sentiments into love.

It's all sales

You can always tell if you are dealing with a real salesperson if they truly believe in the products they are selling. To top that, true salespeople are what they sell. This personal drive is the basis for good results. They transfer the enthusiasm they display towards their product onto their customer. At some point it is inevitable that management, will offer criticism, often for strategic reasons. The salesperson does not understand this because his indomitable enthusiasm is undiminished. However, according to company policy the salesperson has to be controlled. The same once motivated salesperson will change dramatically and will become bothersome.

Selling my department

As part of the Information and Automation Plan the infrastructure of our company was also suitable for third-party usage. We had named this system the Off-brand Banking Concept. The functional and technical infrastructure was highly suited for usage by third parties and in the market this was known and respected.

The downsizing and reorganisation process was well under way and most automation employees were worried and applying for new positions. I knew I had to be clever and I arrived at the thought that it could perhaps be possible to outsource our infrastructure including the staff to an interested party in the market. As far as I knew there were two interested parties in the market that could be interested. I got in touch with them and indeed they were interested.

I told the new Director-general about my plan and he was of course pleased with my idea. I had not expected anything else for it was a cost-effective way to get rid of a number of expensive employees. He authorised me to start negotiations. It soon turned out that I personally became part of the negotiations. There was nothing else for it but to have the Director-general conduct negotiations. Both parties were eager to make me part of the deal.

The good thing about an outsourcing deal is that the personnel involved is still entitled to their full salaries and would be taken over as a whole by the buying party. This concerned foremost the automation staff and it was not easy for them to find another job. It was a good solution as far as my staff was concerned. My solicitor told me it would also be good for me since I was to keep my current salary. In my new position I was to bring in new customers for the shared banking infrastructure.

Personally I was not pleased with the turn of events. I had become a part of deal and I was not able to decide my own future since others were in the process of doing that for me. If I were to back-out of transfer the deal was off, which would be bad for the others. I had no other choice but to accept.

The new Director-general was pleased with the way the outsourcing deal had worked out and he organised a drinks session to celebrate. For me the battle was over and I did not attend. I did not want to raise a toast to someone without any feelings, who treated people badly and without respect. The only cause for celebration he had was the substantial increase of his bonus.

I learned that it is not so bad to lose if you know that you have done everything to win. This was the best I could do for my staff. I just had to accept the fact and try not to get too frustrated.

Losing is not so bad if you are a 100% convinced that you have done everything humanly possible to win. Accepting loss is to be preferred in a new situation and try to make the most of it without feeling frustrated.

Not a sales deal to be proud of

After having ended my dating site subscription I still felt very lonely. It had solved nothing and I had not enjoyed meeting the dating box women. I saw the hurt in their eyes as soon as they realised I was not interested in starting a relationship with them. And the last thing I wanted was to hurt them. Some women were willing to go all the way and stay the night but I just could not do it. I did not want to hurt them the morning after by having to tell them I was not interested in having a relationship with them.

By that time I was convinced that both parties had to fall in love in order to have a fine relationship again. I did have a problem though, because I was very eager to have sex again. I hated the fact that I was out there on the prowl like a hunter for that was definitely not what I wanted.

My daughter's weekend visits grew less frequent. She had her own friends in town. She was always busy and had passed her driving test. Most of her visits served to put her driving skills into practice in my car. It was close to torture, having to give her the keys to my car. She visited her mother even less since she had discovered that her mother was hardly ever at home. Not even on her birthday and mother's day.

Her mother worked on a party boat and was involved in a relationship with the captain/owner of the vessel. It goes without saying that they did not move in together and she was loath to have my daughter find out about the affair for it would have given me ground to stop paying alimony.

I had stopped 'forcing' my daughter to visit her mother. They were both adults now who had to decide for themselves whether they wanted to stay in touch or not. My ex-wife did not seem interested. As a result I was at home alone most weekends.

One Saturday my daughter had taken my car to drive to her house to pick up something. On her return she said, " Dad, do you remember saying you're always having trouble turning in my street because of the lamppost? Well, I found out I have the same problem and now the lamppost has the same colour as your car." I was shocked and stormed outside to have a look. Fortunately it was a just a scrape on the bodywork and easy to polish away. Well, the relationship between men, cars and their daughters is something really special.

I thought I had found a solution for my sexual desires by occasionally contacting an escort girl. I found the selection process exiting and degrading at the same time. But at least if I paid them for their services it did not feel as if I hurt them unnecessary. No emotion involved, and no strings attached. It did not work that way in my case because I always ended up having a conversation with the girl. Their life-stories were without exceptions sad and always evolved around not having any self-esteem or respect for their bodies.

As far as the actual sex was concerned not much happened because I did not find sex without love very satisfying. I gave up on the whole escort business. And in the end it cost me more money than I had bargained for, because all four escort girls I had met I helped to start a new life.

I learned once more that I just could not be cold hearted and selfish. I always felt the need to help others because I felt that was the right thing to do.

It's all sales

Also in sales we recognise this problem. There is this tendency to bow to the customer's will in order to win his approval. 'The customer is always right' and if not, we say he is. A true salesperson can rely on his own knowledge and skills. He is straightforward and not afraid to state his own opinion. This opinion is based on in-depth specialist knowledge. The result is that a customer can extend his knowledge. The customer will appreciate the opinion of the salesperson and will subsequently buy from him.

Dealing with my personal transformation

A software company now employed me and my new manager informed me that it would serve me well if I was to become the Account Manager for one of their major customers (an insurance company). As an Account Manager I could get to know the company, management and my new colleagues better. I had to transform from a decision-maker into an Account Manager who was not involved in the company's decision-making process. Playing at being director was definitely over.

I also remained responsible for the sale of the possibilities concerning the extended infra structure and I had a colleague assigned to me to write a business plan for the sales of this new service.

It was an entirely different world. It soon became clear to me that this software company's main activity was the so called 'body shopping' of computers. That was what they were good at and had been responsible for the considerable growth of the company. All other plans were put on hold if five consultants were not out on an assignment and everybody went back to 'body shopping' again.

Since almost every employee was assigned to a customer during the day, many activities were organised in the evenings. Your presence was of course required because you had to show management you were committed to the company.

The Director-general was a real salesperson. He had surrounded himself with yes-men who did everything he asked. He could get beside himself with rage and would give those present a piece of his mind. He seemed nice, but he really was not. The second managerial level consisted of Account Managers who had no say in the matter. As far as I could determine, managing a company like this was relatively simple when compared to the complex managerial structures of a bank.

It was also pathetic in a sense because on Sunday evening the Director General started sending people e-mails from his home and thereby obliging people to open their mailbox on a Sunday evening. I was having serious doubts about my new position. This feeling was reinforced by the fact that the Director I was to report to kept reminding me that I was earning more money than he did. In response I told him to ask for a raise, but I just knew this situation would not last long.

These were definitely not inspiring surroundings but I decided not to give in but to show them that I could do it. The insurance company, my customer, was a dynamic enterprise offering the opportunity to young managerial talents to develop their skills. I lost no time in establishing good contacts with management and was able to offer advice on automation matters.

Because of the decentralisation I could propagate company policy to the different divisions, which was highly appreciated. This insurance company was capable of adapting continuously to the new developments. I was impressed. I visited this customer as often as I could and talked to people at all levels. I only spent time in my own office when I really had to. In doing so I avoided contact with my own management.

I learned that a full personal transformation was required from Director to Account manager in new surroundings. I had to go out there and visit (prospective) customers and bring in business. I had become a salesperson and that was exactly what I had always tried to avoid.

It's all sales

The art of selling is being able to adapt to new situations. Every (potential) customer requires a different approach. It is this flexibility that separates successful salespeople from the others. It is different, though, when you are demoted. All kinds of processes are involved. On the one hand there is the challenge of getting involved in something new while on the other hand you experience the feeling of having to give something up. As soon as you have made your choice it is essential to come to terms with your feelings and focus on the job in hand for the full 100%. Believe in yourself that you have got what it takes and that you want to be the best. Before you know it you will be back at your old level. Your good fortune will present itself again.

Not listening to the customer

The software company that now employed me was one of the largest in the Netherlands. They were good at the so called 'body shopping' of the computer and that had been the key to their success. Now they wanted to expand by setting up a 'service centre' for their customers and to accomplish this they wanted to in source the systems of their customers while calling it 'co-sourcing'. This new service required a major process of change, which was not easy for management to realise.

For me it was a whole new experience to be employed as a salesperson. I now took a seat at the other side of the negotiating table. I had never pictured myself in this position but I wanted to prove that I could do it. A consultant had been assigned to me who had been a sales executive for the number one hardware supplier in the world. I did not like him for he was arrogant and I did not trust him. He impressed management, though, and I never understood why except for the fact that he was always very submissive to those in charge. I could not help thinking that buttering up the right people surely helped.

One day we were assigned to host a workshop for a prospective customer. It was a midsize bank and it seemed we were onto a serious prospect because a few board members would attend

We had completed our business plan for the service centre and also compiled a presentation for the sales part. The presentation always started with a couple of slides about the company and about our successful position in the market. It was standard material and was always followed by an in-depth outline of the possibilities. Since my colleague was not too knowledgeable about factual matters he always presented the company introduction.

During introductions one of the board members told us that we should skip the slides concerning the company presentation because he did not have a lot of time. He had already gathered that our financial background was solid from reading the financial papers.

My colleague started the presentation and did not skip any of the company slides. The bank director was annoyed, to say the least, and left the conference room after the fifth slide. A terrible situation and I felt ashamed on account of my colleague's behaviour.

I learned that you always have to listen to the customer. I could also perfectly understand the customer's point of view since I had often been in the same position. 'Customer is always king' and wishes to be treated as such.

First rule in sales; listen to the customer. Listen to the information he provides you with and listen to his wishes. There is, however, also another side to the matter. In sales conversations it happens that the customer tells you to skip some of the info because he is in a hurry and wants to know what the price of the product is. If you succumb to this you are definitely entering a danger zone. Selling is nothing but matching the product specifics with the desires and requirements of the customer. If that fits, the price is of secondary importance. If you skip a part of the sales process chances are that the customer will turn down your product. In a case like this it is better to mention the time factor and set up another meeting so the customer can devote more attention to you and your product.

Happy salespeople

Slowly but surely I started to get used to my new position but the cultural differences between a bank and software company are considerable. I had to change into becoming a sales-driven salesperson. I felt more like a customer relation-manager than a real salesperson and I truly believed that effective customer relation management could lead to profitable deals. At my previous employer's I had managed to build an extensive social network without really noticing which I had maintained. In the world of finance, most people knew my name.

I had to sell the usage of consultants, preferably with long-term contracts. If I managed to do this, management was satisfied and I would stay out of trouble.

One day at the office a group of colleagues returned from a customer presentation. They were well pleased and kept slapping each other on the back because as far as they knew they had just given a successful company presentation. They also made sure the Director-general was aware of their successful visit and he congratulated them with a job well done.

I also congratulated them and at the same time asked them for the name of the company. It turned out that I was quite familiar with the bank they mentioned and I also asked them whether a good friend of mine, the Automation Manager, had been present. The answer was affirmative since he had been chairing the meeting.

Back at my desk I received a phone call from my friend the Automation Manager who had been at the receiving end of the presentation. He asked me whether it was true this company now employed me. When I told him this was the case he told this was the worst presentation he had ever witnessed in his life. He advised me to go and look for another job because this company was not worth my while. He asked me to pass the message on to management.

I went to see the Director-general and told him about the telephone conversation. I was dumbfounded by his reaction because his response was a typical case of 'shooting the messenger'. He was not at all pleased and made some unfriendly remarks about my friend, the bank's Automation Manager.

I learned that it is not important what a supplier thinks about a presentation, but that it is much more important to determine what the customer thinks.

People are often self-centred. Many speakers are preoccupied with themselves instead of with their audience and the actual message. Because of being preoccupied with yourself your are not focussed on the actual message and your audience. Your feelings are of secondary importance.

Selling is not always the fun it is made out to be

As the Account Manager of a major insurance company for a software company I was also responsible for all its subsidiaries. I had decided to visit them all to determine whether we could do business together.

One of my young and dynamic colleagues, also a member of the sales team, usually accompanied me on those visits. This visit was to be different because my colleague told me that this company was not pleased with us. My company had carried out a project in the past, which had failed. It had cost the company a huge amount of money and my company had not been willing to accept any responsibility, hence their dissatisfaction.

In spite of this negative setting I felt we had to pay them a visit to see whether we could overcome past differences and make a fresh start. It was, after all, bad for my company to have a dissatisfied customer spreading the word.

It was quite a long drive but my colleague and I left in good spirits. My colleague was always asking after my daughter and I told him that I was not a fool and would therefore never introduce her to him. I liked him because he was clever and eager to learn. Unfortunately, he had suffered from burnout at an early age. As a result whenever he felt stress reaching an unacceptable level he would back out. This did not happen in a natural fashion, though. He just disappeared. That is how he avoided stressful situations. It did worry me because I wondered what the future consequences of his behaviour would be.

Still in high spirits we were led into the Director's office but he did not accept our handshake and gave us an angry look. In addition we were not offered coffee and he started off with the rendition of a long list of complaints, reproaches and frustrations from the past about company management and the quality of our work.

He was genuinely angry and frustrated. Slowly but surely we changed our behaviour and were no longer the cheerful salespeople on a mission. We sat there and listened intently. I was ashamed of my company and for what we had done, or rather had failed to do. It could not have been worse. At the end of his story he told us that had been was determined to receive us because he wanted us to hear his story. I understood his frustrations perfectly and I offered him on behalf of my company my sincere apologies while looking him straight in the eye. I meant it and I thought it was the least we could do. He accepted my apologies and on our departure he did accept my handshake.

When we drove back to the office my young colleague told me that he had not expected the kind of behaviour I had displayed at the customer's office. He found it amazing that I was capable of humbling myself for the benefit of a customer. It surprised him, but he respected it at the same time.

On our return from our trip I told the Director-general what had happened. He just shrugged his shoulders and told me he never liked that director anyway. I now understood the director's frustrations even better. My manager had been responsible for the project and had never even deemed it appropriate to offer his apologies.

I learned that I was capable of looking at problems from two different angles and assess them objectively. I also understood the customer's predicament for I had been a customer myself and I had experienced the same problems. The customer in the story above could sense this.

It's all sales

A conversation without proper introductions is on the whole doomed to fail. When an awkward situation arises it is worthwhile to raise the issue first for it will clear the air. If this is dealt with, the road will be clear to make a fresh start.

Knowledge does not always sell

The Director-general introduced me to an attractive woman. She had been invited to carry out research into the possibilities of selling a new product on the Internet. She was to interview me on account of my banking knowledge.

She was very intelligent with a combined University degree but could also be described as someone out of control. For at the slightest excuse she was distracted from the matter in hand. During a meeting she could all of a sudden start talking about the flower design on the wallpaper and on other occasions she could sink her teeth into a problem. She was definitely special and a fun person to be with. However, when it came to doing business, she was a disaster.

We got on well together and she told me a lot about her personal life. Her story was also a garbled one. She had been married to a professional soccer player for one day, she had given birth to a daughter while she had always believed to be infertile. She had been employed as a bank manager with a mid sized bank and had left it with a golden handshake. It was an incredible story but very interesting to listen to.

She had a brilliant mind and was able to initiate innovative products of which others took advantage on a regular basis. Usually they would invite her to carry out research without paying her for it. If her ideas turned out to be inapplicable they thanked her for her efforts and would introduce her ideas as soon as she was out of the picture. I felt that on too many occasions people were taking advantage of her and I tried to help by coaching her.

The same thing happened to her at my company. Once more her ideas were not implemented and they thanked her for her time and effort. For three months she had put in an awful lot of work without getting anything in return. I could not abide the fact that people treated her so badly.

And of course she was partly to blame for it as well. She had to change her style and become a professional. I discussed the matter with her and she asked whether I would be willing to manager her affairs. I promised to help her out, because I felt she deserved it.

I offered her help on both business and private matters and I also made sure she attended some haptonomy sessions to restore the balance between mind and body... I also advised her on how to raise her daughter. We became and still are good friends.

I learned that 'brain picking' can be difficult to prove especially when it concerns small companies without means to protect themselves.

The lady described above is a visual thinker. Visual thinkers are people who think in images. Everything they talk about they see in pictures. It is crystal clear to them what it is all about. They often experience difficulties, though, in trying to put into words what they mean. They talk fast and skip words, which leads to them being misunderstood. Another character trait associated with visual thinkers is being sensitive to impulses from their surroundings. They ramble from one subject to another and leave a chaotic impression. Communicating with these people is most effective when you try to make your point by means of a little sketch. Visualise things …

How not to sell a joint enterprise

To transform a software company specialised in the so-called 'body shopping' of computers into a software company also exploiting 'competence centres' was not an easy task. By 'in sourcing' myself and also the systems I had developed for my former employer they now thought they had a starting point to try and contact customers who would be interested in using the system. At least, that is what they told us.

In order to realise this, a project manager had been appointed to compile a business plan. I was a member of the project team but I did not particularly like the Project Manager. He did not know the first thing about banking and abused my knowledge to score points with management. I had not been able to work out exactly what his assignment was but shortly afterwards one of the standard systems, the Switch, including the customer contracts were sold to a former competitor. Had this been agreed beforehand? I will never know, but there was nothing I could do but accept it.

All that was left was the Standard Banking system. This software company, however, had a bad relationship with the supplier of the Standard Banking System. They had embarked on a joint enterprise with a bank that had failed, leaving them to blame each other. In order to have the "Competence Centre" sell the Off-brand Banking Concept successfully a good relationship with the supplier, my friends, was essential. The business plan would be useless without the support of the supplier.

I warned company management but they would not listen. They filed an order to freeze the supplier's assets (seven banks) in the Netherlands.

My friend, the charismatic Director of the supplying company was enraged and phoned me because he wanted to discuss matters with my Director-general in order to solve the conflict. That is exactly what happened, for the Director-general and I went to meet them.

The charismatic Director offered us lunch and during lunch we drank the most expensive wine I ever had before in my entire life (a Pomerol). He even ordered a second bottle and on the way home on the plane I stopped myself from going to the toilet. This wine was just too expensive to waste by urinating in an aeroplane toilet.

The two directors managed to come to an agreement and had the freeze of assets lifted. Unfortunately there had not been enough time to discuss the future of the 'Competence centre". Still, by that time I had known the charismatic Director of the supplier for quite a while and I was convinced that he would never forget let alone forgive what my Director-general had done. He would never trust him again, that was part of his character.

The ideas and plans for the "Banking Competence Centre" never amounted to anything because there was no support from the supplier. It goes without saying that nobody was to blame and nobody was responsible.

I learned once more that before you take action you need to determine first what the consequences of those actions are. Especially in an international environment where you also have to deal with cultural differences, you need to make sure you know what the consequences are.

It's all sales

Up to a certain extent we all use our intuition in everything we do. Experience teaches us that, among other things, we are driven by the perceptions we have of others. These perceptions can get in the way when dealing with people from different cultures. This already starts with differences between people from different districts, let alone with people from other countries. Because of differences in idioms, sayings and use of colloquialisms it is quite a challenge to find out exactly what they mean. Asking questions is better than making assumptions.

Honesty does not always sell

The company I worked for was in the habit of organising an annual business trip to an exotic destination. This year they had planned a trip to South Africa and since I was the Account Manager for one of their most important customers, I was invited as well. Quite a few friends of members of the Board of Directors would join us, of course.

In South Africa we visited a bank where they showed us their decision room. They had access to a lot of information about their offices and market environment of these offices. In a room they had appointed sixteen computer screens. The members of the board of a bank were invited into this room and they would discuss the (financial) results of that particular affiliate.

Every screen showed not only their results but also those of the competition. If a bank director would argue that they were short staffed they would show the actual state of affairs on the screen and the number of staff the competition employed etc. etc. Every excuse a manager could come up with would be invalidated in this way by presenting the actual facts on one of the screens. They must have felt pretty uncomfortable being invited into this room.

I could not help but realise how much information was needed for this approach and where this information could be gained. Yet, in this country a director was still the boss and employees were forced to keep track of their time and hand in detailed reports. It did make things a lot easier and I was truly impressed.

And no trip to South Africa would be complete without a game drive. We went to the game park first thing in the morning and it was absolutely fantastic to see these beautiful animals in their natural surroundings. I was enthralled by the wonders of nature and appalled by the mess human beings had made of it.

A social outing was also included in the programme so we went to Soweto to visit a school. We went there in blinded vans but on our arrival many children and quite a few 'Big Mamas' greeted us. The first thing that struck me was that everybody seemed happy and looked cheerful.

The women sang their songs and played with the children on their laps. We entered the building and were invited to share a meal with them. Next, we were seated with the women in a classroom.

As a part of the visit we were to introduce ourselves and the first in line told them he was a bank director. They women yelled 'give us money, you have money'. After that he could not avoid pledging some money. The second director told him he was single to which the women answered that they all wanted to marry him and come with him.

Those following had learned their lesson by that time and forgot to mention that a bank employed them and all of a sudden they had all been blessed with a wife and many, many children. This in order to avoid problems with the 'Big Mamas'. When we left Soweto we made a generous donation towards the school on behalf of all of us.

From this trip I learned that people living in poverty can by happy as well, but that money is still important. The difference between rich and poor and black and white was too big and led to many problems. Being completely honest is sometimes not an option but salespeople never lie, they just happen to omit a few facts.

It's all sales

In sales lying is unacceptable. There are, however, many salespeople who think they may miss out on an order if they tell their customer the whole truth. It happens often enough that a salesperson holds back a few delivery specifications or tells a customer that they can deliver within a week, while they know that is not feasible. Do not lie, just bend the message to your advantage.

The most successful enterprises

I had become a true salesperson. I had never expected this to happen and I had always told those around me that I would never become a salesperson. I had had my fair share of dealing with salespeople in the past. Some of them I liked, but most of them I did not like because they were not really interested in my company and our business. All they were interested in was in getting a result and nothing else.

That was not the kind of salesperson I wanted to turn into. I wanted to get to know the customer, their products and I wanted them to improve with the help of my products and in doing so creating a win-win situation. I intended to become a customer relation manager rather than a real salesperson. I believed my approach was the right one and I did not really care whether management agreed with me or not.

I just had to accept it and from a spiritual point of view it was important that I just let things happen, go with the flow and not resist the turn of events. To go with the flow of life would be good for me.

I did everything I could to acquire both theoretical and practical knowledge about this new part that I was to play. I read many books about sales and talked quite often with friends in my network about sales and its importance to companies.

One of the books I read was about successful companies and the funny thing was that most of them no longer existed. Together with my friends I analysed this phenomenon and in most cases we came to the conclusion that a managerial problem had been the cause of the collapse of these enterprises.

I enjoyed these discussions and I learned a lot from them. It reminded me of a beautiful story from the Bible about the seven fat and the seven lean years. But without sales a company simply could not survive and the ability to keep up with market changes and to stay ahead of the competition was not an easy matter. Innovation and the ability to make decisions are essential for a company. Starting up a company is a whole different ball game than consolidating an enterprise and expanding requires a different type of management and a different approach.

Examples of companies that are capable of change are of course IBM and Philips. In a successful sports team they also change trainer (leader) about every five years. Surviving companies still seek innovation even when times are bad.

I learned a lot about sales through reading and by talking about the business of selling and customer relation management. It was my way of trying to turn it into something that would suit me. Making a deal was great. Another new challenge in my life.

Something every salesperson needs to do every now and again is to check whether his approach still works. Even though one salesperson is more susceptible to challenges while the other would rather stick to the system he knows, it is up to Sales Management to determine the right approach, for in a sales team both types will be present. By communicating properly with your salespeople you can discover their strong suits and use them to advantage. When people are appointed in the right position and are happy in their job, it will generate energy for them to use to do their job properly. The good thing is that as soon as people experience a sense of flow, luck is on their side. Call it enforcing coincidence.

A new role and a new approach

My new role as a salesperson in a business environment proved to be quite demanding. Not only did I have to get used to a new position I also had to change from being a Director and Automation Manager into a successful salesperson. Aiming for success was in my blood. I wanted to win and to be the best and I was willing to make sacrifices in order to achieve that. I realised that I could only win if I was able to transform successfully into a salesperson. I decided to devote a lot of time and energy to this.

On a business level I knew what to do. There were plenty of books around on the role of a salesperson, techniques and methods. And of course I now benefited from the fact that over the past years I had met a large number of salespeople and I had already determined what kind of salesperson I wanted to become. It is like in soccer. You can only become a proper defender if you have been a striker before.

After my divorce I was still alone. My daughter was independent now and was doing well. I had many friends I could go out with to concerts and parties. I also enjoyed spending the weekends by myself with my books and music or take a relaxing bath with a single malt whisky. I immersed myself into spiritual matters and went with some of my female friends to 'readings' and 'healings'. This enabled me to get to know myself better.

One remarkable thing I did in that period was attending a presentation by Wayne Dyer. I had never before spent three hours listening in stunned silence to somebody else. I was impressed beyond words. Could life be lived in such a beautiful and simple fashion?

Well, why not and from then on I would try to make something special out of every day and enjoy it. The past was over and you could not change that and you did not know what the future would hold. Today is a beautiful new day and you had to enjoy it. I learned to rest whenever necessary and I felt the desire to turn into an intuitive person.

The balance between rest and activity was vital to me and once more I felt capable of smiling and being cheerful the whole day. I knew when to 'peak' and when it was not really necessary. Take life as it offers itself, follow your own feelings and dare to rely on them, that is what it was all about. This approach generated a lot of energy and I wanted to use the energy to become a good person and be good to others, especially those around me.

I did not feel the need to donate money to charities since I never could be quite sure about what would happen with the money. No, helping people around me who really needed it, that made much more sense. You can also be poor in a rich country. I wanted to use my energy to help and coach young people on a private as well as on a business level.

Using my life-experience and my belief in God it was actually just letting nature run its course. It was simply a case of more mature people coaching the next generation towards the future. I did not harbour any ill feelings towards anyone and always tried to see the positive side. This approach made me feel positive. And in actual fact this had been my approach to life before but on a more subconscious level.

I learned to accept myself for what I was. I was a giver and not a receiver. It was also clear that self-knowledge had come to me because life had not been easy. Still, when the going gets tough, the tough get going.

It's all sales

If you are capable of introspection it will this will provide you with the tools to improve. It is essential to keep remembering the successes for they will stimulate you and help securing a repeat performance.

Not investing is not selling

All account managers had to compile a business plan for their customer. I organised a number of brainstorming sessions with my team in order to determine the possibilities and challenges regarding this major insurance company and its subsidiaries. I enjoyed working on a business plan for a customer. I knew that the only thing management wanted to hear from me was whether we could generate more business by means of selling more "hands". This was not good enough as far as I was concerned for I was determined to write a complete business plan including every possible option.

I had built up a good relationship with the Automation Director of the insurance company. Automation had been decentralised to the separate business units, but he was still responsible for strategic matters and setting company policy with a small team of professionals. He was also still in charge of the computer centre.

At business unit level the managers were responsible for the projects and automation budgets. This also included the subsidiaries, which I visited on a regular basis.

I had discussed their strategy and policy at length with the Automation Director and I understood and supported their policy whenever I visited business unit management and subsidiaries. This director appreciated my attitude and was therefore always more than willing to confer with me.

Their policy focussed on outsourcing. It was their intention to outsource their computer centre and legacy systems because the old systems took up too much automation support thereby blocking innovation opportunities. The outsourcing scheme for the computer centre had already been initiated.

I made an appointment with the Automation Director to discuss our business plan. He told me that one of his major frustrations was that my software company was always eager to send an invoice for their efforts but was never willing to invest. He would appreciate it tremendously if both companies could embark on a joint enterprise, sharing the risks and investments. We defined an innovative project and would start up a preliminary survey on a 50/50 cost basis. After the preliminary survey a project would be initiated to the benefit of both parties.

It offered an excellent opportunity for us and it was subsequently included in the business plan. We also predicted that this combined project would generate a lot of work for both companies by means of the outsourcing of legacy systems. If we could prove that we were willing to make the investments they would seriously consider us as an outsourcing partner. After all, we were already preferred supplier. My team and I considered it an exciting challenge.

We submitted the business plan to my manager and after a couple of days he told me he had never seen such a good business plan before. Naturally, we were pleased and my team and I went out to dinner to celebrate the successful outcome.

I learned that I enjoyed playing the part of mediator between the customer and the company I worked for. I was made for this part and I had been doing the same over the years in different positions. Always aiming for a win-win situation.

It's all sales

A salesperson serves as an intermediary between the customer and his own employer. The task he is set to perform is to manage the affairs of the customer within the product range of his own company as well as possible. That is the only option to create customer loyalty. Still, not every company management adheres to this vision. Some think salespeople should not bend too much towards a customer. A healthy internal discussion on this topic never hurts.

Selling a business plan

At first I found it hard getting used to being an employee of a software company. After having been employed by banks, joining the IT cowboys involved a major transformation. Unfortunately this transition had not come about out of my own free will because I had been part of an outsourcing deal that also included my staff and automation systems.

I was not really impressed by the management of the software company. The Director-general was an excellent salesperson but a bad Director-general who had himself surrounded by yes-men. If something went wrong he would swear and throw abuse at his staff, especially in the presence of others. I did not have a lot of respect for the Director-general as a human being.

My direct manager was young and well educated but whenever I came across him he always mentioned the fact that I earned more money than he did. I always responded by telling him that it was his problem and he should make sure that he got paid what he thought he deserved. It never felt right, though. I wanted to prove to myself and to them that I was worth every penny I earned and that I was well suited for the position of Account Manager.

I thought the best opportunity to do this presented itself when we had to compile a business plan for our customer. I regarded it as an opportunity to convince management that I could generate profit and I felt backed by the good relationship I had with my customer. I was convinced that my customer expressed the same opinion to my management.

Still, somehow I sensed it was too good to be true. One day the Director-general called me on account of some problems with one of my customer's subsidiaries. He was swearing and cursing at me for no apparent reason and blamed me for everything while I did not even know what the problem was. In the past he had been responsible for this particular customer and now it seemed as if I was going to be successful where he had failed. He did not like that one bit. Being sworn at is not a pleasant experience.

I still clung to the notion that my manager had told me the business plan was the best he had ever seen. Good thing we had put so much effort in that. I could not shake off this uncomfortable feeling and I was already looking at other job openings. There was this small Interim Management Company that was very willing to hire me and appoint me as Interim Manager or Project Manager.

As the end of the financial year drew nearer the annual appraisals were due. When I arrived at the office I learned much to my surprise that my appraisal interview was to be conducted by the Director-general and not only my direct manager. This was not according to standard procedures and all sorts of alarm bells went off inside my head.

During the interview the Director-general did all the talking while my manager did not say a word but supported him by means of his body language. The Director-general ran the business plan completely into the ground and was not at all willing to invest. It also turned out that all of a sudden my manager had conveniently forgotten his previous praise for the plan. I tried to look him in the eye while all this was going on but he averted his eyes. It slowly dawned upon me that money was what all this bashing was about. They wanted to lower my salary and instead of bringing that out into the open they had decided to try and take me down a peg or two. I did not respond. I just looked at them and left the room without saying a word.

The whole procedure had left me feeling miserable and I went home straight away. I was not about to let them start treating me like this for I did not deserve it. I made up my mind and that night I had dinner with the Director-general of the Interim Management bureau and I signed the employment contract on the spot. That same night I wrote my letter of resignation and sent it by e mail and regular mail to the company's management. It was such a relief.

The only response I ever got from the Director-general was that he never expected me to react this way and that it had never been his intention to have me leave the company. I just looked at him. He cast his eyes to the ground and never said another word to me.

Still, I did experience a sense of gratitude towards this company because by employing me they had enabled me to transform from a bank director into a salesperson.

I had learned a great deal this year and fortunately I had the ability to put the situation into proper perspective and respond accordingly. I was not going to let anyone humiliate me and I still believed in my principles and myself.

No matter how good your product or service is, if the customer is involved in internal conflicts no deals will be made. It is much better to see whether you can help the customer with good advice. Someone on the outside can take better stock of a situation because he is not involved. Offering helicopter view is essential to those who are personally involved. The customer will remember your good advice and will remain a loyal customer.

Selling without speaking a single word

Once again I had to master a new role, the role of Interim Manager. I was employed by a small agency together with about twenty other professional Interim Managers. Company policy aimed at providing companies experiencing difficulties with an Interim Manager or Project Manager. The Interim or Project Manager was expected to solve the problem by means of being a neutral mediator between all parties involved. On completion of the job another job would be waiting with another company. I appreciated this neutral part because I believed it was essential when it came down to solving problems.

They had also hired me to generate more business through my network in the finance sector since they felt they were not sufficiently represented in that industry. This was not easy to achieve since most financial businesses were bound to a "Master Agreement" with the major software companies they could not breach. I considered it a personal challenge to do something about that.

After having spent a month at the office in order to get to know my new colleagues, one of the directors approached me because he wanted me to accompany him on an intake at a scientific institution that carried out many assignments for the government and the army.

This institution, which employed some of the most brilliant 'Whiz-kids' in the country, had to privatise and was looking for an Interim Manager to reorganise their General and Technical Services Department. Since I had been responsible for a similar department with a previous employer I seemed suited for the job.

It became clear that the manager that accompanied me had been on good terms with this institution for a long time and had carried out several jobs as a Project Manager himself. I had adjusted my CV slightly for the occasion and together we had a meeting with the Director-general.

No matter what the outcome of the meeting would be, as far as I was concerned I would take the job on one condition. No forced redundancies. I never quite pictured myself as a relentless reorganiser. I definitely did not want to get involved in this kind of proceedings due to bad experiences with a previous employer.

It was an incredible interview. The Director-general did all the talking and was solely preoccupied with his own plans for the future. It was a 'one man show' with us performing the part of audience. The General and Technical Services department nor my part in the scheme of things was mentioned once. I knew only an hour was allotted for this meeting so after about fifty minutes I interrupted him politely and asked him whether any forced redundancies were expected. He replied that was not the case and continued his monologue.

On our way back to the office my director told me I should not have interrupted the Director-general. This was how he always conducted interviews and he did not know the first thing about the General and Technical Services Department because he was not interested in it. All his meetings and interviews were conducted in the same fashion simply because he was too preoccupied with his plans for the future.

A day later they phoned us and told me I was hired for the job. The Director-general had been satisfied by the interview. I was about to embark on this job with all these 'Whiz-kids''. Before I was to start, my family and I were screened as part of the security policy of this company.

I learned that I did not always have to sell myself; others could handle the conversation as well.

It's all sales

A sales conversation does not always go as planned. The most important thing in sales is the relationship between the salesperson and the customer. If the customer enjoys discussing other matters with you, why stop him? The customer is very well aware of the fact that getting a result is the name of the game. At one point I was involved in a conversation in which the customer talked for about fifty minutes about issues that mattered to him. Only in the final stages of the conversation did he sign the order.

Selling a reorganisation

The first thing I did was writing a master plan relating to the reorganisation of the General and Technical Services Department. Included in the master plan were the starting points for the reorganisation and I had already submitted the plan for approval to the Board of Directors. Next, I had compiled seven project plans with the help of all those involved and the seven projects were implemented in sequence according to the master plan.

The whole issue was not really complicated and by just using common sense I was perfectly able to determine what was required to carry out their assignments at reduced costs. While I was drawing up a statement of affairs I had come across reports compiled by predecessors that already indicated what needed to be done. At first I did not understand why they needed me to do what seemed obvious.

It did not take look for me to discover that the 'Whiz-kids' were good at writing reports but absolutely ill suited to bring about changes. This company obviously also had its share of managerial problems. That was one reason why not much had been done so far, but as far as I could see there had to be other reasons.

Through all the interviews I conducted with those involved I found out what the crux of the matter was. It turned out that eight of the eleven members of the Works Council worked in the General and Technical Services Department. The Director-general did not feel secure in trying to implement changes because he feared the Works Council would oppose the plans. I had my task cut out for me and I could start the 'selling process'.

I discussed my plans with every single individual involved and also with the members of the Works Council. I tried to convince them of the fact that the measures had to be taken in order to continue the process of privatisation. Next, I included all eight members of the Works Council in my project organisation. Nothing happened without them knowing about it. And I knew that gradually they started to like and respect me.

Still the plans required formal approval by the Works Council. I had been invited to their meeting with the Director-general. He was rather nervous but I managed to convince him of a successful outcome since I was certain that the plans would meet with approval. In a sense I understood the Director-general's attitude for he was only interested in his plans for the future and not in the mundane aspects of running the business.

Fortunately no forced redundancies were required and a suitable solution would be found for all those involved.

After my presentation the Works Council voted in favour of the plans, much to the relief of the Director-general who was grateful to me. In order to implement the plans I knew I could depend on the support of the Board of Directors and the Works Council. From there on it was a piece of cake.

I learned that there are huge differences between scientists and pragmatic thinking people. To each his own. It was also important not to avoid important problems but to deal with them head-on and to involve the right people in a process of change.

It's all sales

In sales things are not very different. A mistake many salespeople make is that when wanting to do business at top level you forget about those having to live with the outcome of the plans. Many salespeople have short-term considerations only. Being awarded the order is the most important thing. Yet, if you do not inform those at the lower levels within the organisation this may come back to haunt you in the future. Very often the motives of those in lower positions are irrational; meaning they are not susceptible to arguments that are relevant to company management. A profitable deal with a different coffee supplier was sabotaged because the canteen lady would no longer be able to collect the saving stamps.

Bad selling by a supplier

My first job as an Interim Manager was to reorganise the General and Technical Services Department of a well-known Dutch company. In order to bring about substantial cost reductions I had defined seven projects and had written seven project plans with the help of those directly involved.

I was now responsible for the General and Technical Services Department and the previous manager of this department reported to me. He was not pleased with this, and I could relate to that. I treated him with respect and I discussed all my plans with him openly. By doing so I tried to convince him of the necessity of the imminent changes.

My responsibilities included the cleaning of the premises. I had received many complaints from those dissatisfied with the cleaning process. Things were a bit complicated because the cleaning process had been partly subcontracted to a cleaning agency, but we also employed our own cleaning staff. A halfway measure that proved to be insufficient since the previous head of the General and Technical Services Department also felt responsible for the external cleaners. All this to the advantage of the cleaning agency that was well paid for their efforts and was not responsible for managerial matters in spite of being paid handsomely for that.

I decided to call the manager of the cleaning agency and invite him to an interview. I made sure I sounded a bit surly on the phone when I invited him for a visit. I also told him about the change in management of the department and asked him to visit the next day at 11 a.m.

The next day he called me at 10.30 and told me he would be late because of heavy traffic. I did not believe him and I checked the Internet to see whether there were any traffic jams. There were not any in his part of the country. At 11 a.m. he contacted me once more to tell me he would be at least forty-five minutes late. I told him that if that was the case he would have only fifteen minutes left to talk to me, because I had another important meeting where my presence was required (which was not true).

He was led into my office at 11.45 and I did not offer him any coffee but told him in no uncertain terms that I was particularly displeased with the quality of their cleaning and that I was considering terminating the contract. He was obviously shocked and I think he had underestimated my new position and assignment.

When I arrived at the company restaurant for lunch I saw him having lunch together with the previous Manager of the General and Technical Services

Department. As it turned out they were good friends and it was obvious they now had a lot to discuss over lunch.

I learned that this supplier did not take me seriously in my capacity of manager. His friend the previous Manager of the General and Technical Services Department probably had not properly informed him. And of course it is never easy having to tell your friends that you are no longer in charge. By addressing him in the way I had, I hoped it was clear that I intended to run a tight ship.

It's all sales

The story above is an obvious example of underestimating a customer, for a customer should never be taken for granted. As a supplier you will have to prove time and again that your product or service is the best option for your customer. The most important element is effectual communication. The right amount of visits, e-mails and phone calls will do the trick.

Being 'bought' by a friend

When a software company as part of an outsourcing deal had hired me, the Director of one of our major suppliers called me. It was the charismatic Director of the supplier of our standard banking system. In addition to the fact that I had been responsible for the buying and implementation of the banking system, I had also served as a reference customer and I had been the co-founder of the user-group. The outsourcing deal had come to his attention and he had told me then that I had been his best salesperson and if I ever needed a job I only had to call him and he would offer me a job for life. At the time I could not accept his offer because I did not want to let down those who were also part of the outsourcing deal.

He contacted me once more and told me that as part of a contract with a new customer he had to open a new affiliate in the Netherlands. He was direct in his approach and asked me whether I would be inclined to undertake this for him and his company. He asked me to send him an e-mail with my salary conditions. Next, he invited me to dinner at one of the most expensive hotels in the city to discuss his proposal. I felt really positive about it all.

When I met him at the hotel it felt good to be able to greet each other as old friends. He had put his financial proposition in a PowerPoint presentation and it was an absolutely fantastic offer. The position on offer was that of Country Manager/ Customer Relation Manager and also build the affiliate from scratch. A great challenge, which would also signal the start of my international career. It was an offer I simply could not refuse.

There was one problem remaining, though. Because the Interim Management Company that employed me had been good to me and I wanted to leave in an appropriate manner. Since they had not yet invested any money in me and I had already done a job as an Interim Manager I had already generated some money for the company. I decided to bring the matter out into the open and they could do nothing but agree with me that it was an offer I just could not refuse. They were, however, sorry to see me go. I promised them that whenever possible I would promote their services in my network.

I had known most of the people at the company I was to join for years. It was a bit like a homecoming. I was to sign the contract during the Christmas and New-Year's party at a very stylish venue in London. All those employed by the company had been invited and had come from all over the world to join the party in London.

My friend, the charismatic Director, held his Christmas speech and told those present that on that very day his best salesperson had signed a contract. He asked me to rise and I was greeted by a standing ovation from my new colleagues. This reception sent shivers down my spine because I had never experienced anything like it. I made me happy and I felt good about this sudden turn of events.

Well, I soon realised that when the Director said from scratch, he meant from scratch. In addition to two main offices they only had one affiliate abroad. The first thing I decided to do was to rent temporary office space and start writing a business plan.

We already had six customers in the Netherlands and I visited them all to ask them what they expected from this local office and from me. In fact, I already knew the answer to these questions. They wanted a better helpdesk, better maintenance and better support.

I started the job in a rented office and at first the only person to visit me was our Sales Manager. For the first time in my life I had to write every single thing in the English language. My e-mails and business plan had to be written in English. Since I had no gift for languages this took a lot of effort at first. Whenever I apologised to my colleagues they responded by 'don't worry we understand what you're going on about anyway'. The gathered the missing bits from my body language.

After about three months I thought I had managed to overcome most of the language problems and I confidently said to my English colleague, the Sales Manager, that I thought my English had improved considerably. Without looking up from his laptop he replied "Do you think so?" I landed back on earth again.

I learned that after years of hard work I was finally, and much later than expected, rewarded for all my efforts. Finally I was appreciated and I appreciated the fact that I was. That night, alone in my hotel room, I thanked my God.

The moments that you will always remember because they left a lasting impression can be used for the rest of your life. When you end up in a difficult situation or when you have to deal with a difficult interview you can think back of your successful moment and use them. Whenever you feel tense and troubled about what you have to do, think back of your successes. Allow the emotions you experienced at the time back into your mind. You will regain your strength and will gain confidence. You will exude confidence when you enter an office.

The best restaurant in town

This restaurant was located in the city centre. It was a Chinese restaurant and it been elected best restaurant in the city for many years in a row.

Together with a business friend I decided to pay this restaurant a visit. We had not made any reservations since that was not possible, and on our arrival we had to wait in line for our turn. People even had to wait outside. Curious and hungry we decided to take a chance and wait our turn.

As soon as we were allowed to enter the building it was more like a company canteen than an actual restaurant. It held simple tables and chairs and featured tiles on the walls. But the place was packed to the roof with diners. The restaurant had two kitchens, one at the back and one at the front of the restaurant.

We were allocated a table and as soon as we sat down a Chinese waiter approached us and handed us a menu that resembled the complete works of a prolific author. He did not say anything and was even a bit unfriendly. As far as the food was concerned anything was possible but friends had recommended the oysters and the Peking duck. Both dishes were famous throughout the country. They waiter stopped by at our table and took our order and whenever we named a dish he was able to come up with the number on the menu. He had actually memorised all 400 dishes and their numbers. "You want drink?" he asked and we ordered Chinese tea for two.

Two minutes later he brought the tea and plunged it unceremoniously on our table. We had to pour it ourselves. Another couple of minutes later he brought along one starter. As it turned out they just brought out the dishes as they had been prepared. My oysters arrived about five minutes later and I had not finished when he already turned up with the next main course, the Peking duck. All dishes were more or less hurled onto our table without a word. But the food was exquisite and of excellent quality so we enjoyed our meal.

As soon as we had finished they cleared the table and were we presented with the bill, without having asked for it. And it was incredible the modest amount of money we had to pay for this excellent meal. We had to pay up quickly because the next in line was after our table. After an hour we were already outside and went for coffee elsewhere.

I learned that when the product is good and price/quality ratio is as well, the product will sell itself. And in order to enjoy this we just had to accept that we were treated in what seemed an unfriendly manner. The behaviour of the Chinese waiter is standard Chinese behaviour. It seems unfriendly but it is not. This restaurant obviously relied on turnover and many customer sessions per night.

In Western society this is a different concept, high quality at a low price and low service level. This is acceptable in supermarkets but uncommon for restaurants. Having dinner at a restaurant is more than just feeding yourself. We want to be entertained and waited on hand and foot. But if one of the variables of the marketing mix is exceptionally high we are willing to adjust our standards. We accept not being treated properly, having to wait for a long time, having your dishes served at different times simply because the food is exquisite. Even if the price had been higher, it still would have been accepted. In Europe we have shops and other outlets with a low service level, which is accepted as long as the prices remain competitive.

Selling as a Country Manager

Management had approved my business plan for the set-up of a local affiliate. My manager was pleased and I could go ahead with trying to find suitable premises, decide on the interior design and most importantly, recruit staff. I enjoyed carrying out the many different tasks.

In my business plan I had indicated that recruitment would not be an easy matter because candidates would have to sign a standard employment contract that did not offer the benefits included in Dutch employment contracts.

Yet, I did decide to call some of my former colleagues who were familiar with the Standard Banking System and to inform whether they were willing to come and work for us. I was pleasantly surprised when most of them agreed. Almost everyone I approached wanted to come and join the company in spite of the fact we were not able to offer the favourable conditions. In no time I had managed to put together a team of twelve people.

When it came to the interior of the new office space, the wife of the charismatic Director helped us out. She was in charge of selecting the standard furniture and the interior design of the local offices. I liked her and we got into the habit of talking about our children and life in general. We became good friends.

One of the points of improvement as indicated by the employees was to instigate the set up of a functional helpdesk. One of my colleagues wanted to take on that responsibility but our international helpdesk was situated in India and communication did not exactly go smoothly.

I decided to go to India together with my colleague to pay a visit to the international helpdesk and improve communication. For both of us this was our first visit to India and we were very impressed by what we saw. It was incredible and very impressive to witness first hand what was possible in such a densely populated country like India.

We visited the temple of Sheba, the Goddess. Barefoot and with a red dot positioned on our forehead (at a price) we walked around the 'tree of love' right at the heart of the temple. Since we both did not know who the true God in our life was, and what to call him, we decided it would not hurt if all the Gods liked us.

The business results of our face-to-face meeting with the helpdesk in India were phenomenal. Communication improved dramatically and after a while even our most demanding customer had to admit he no longer had anything to complain about and was happy with our service.

It felt good to be together again with all these ex colleagues and we organised an outing every month to encourage team building.

I learned that people were also willing to work for people they respected and trusted. Benefits are no longer important. And I realised after my visit to India that I most certainly had been born and that I lived in one of the most privileged parts of the world. I thanked my God for that.

It's all sales

Not only employees feel better if they are happy and feel 'at home' at the company they work for. Customers also feel better if they are comfortable with a supplier. Hence the importance of a good relationship with your customer A customer should be pleased to see you at every visit. If you also happen to show up with a well-prepared story, success guaranteed.

Personal coach to a young woman

For my visit to India I needed vaccinations. During my visit to the health centre I met a young female employee and we started talking. She was open and enthusiastic and I gave her my business card and asked her to call me so we could get to know each other better.

Because of my trip to India I had already forgotten about the meeting when she finally called me. We agreed to meet at my place. She sat down on the couch and started talking about her life and at one point she continued her story whilst sitting on the floor. We were very at ease with each other and she could sense that I was genuinely interested in her. We met on several occasions.

Her life story touched me deeply. As a young girl she was raised by her grandmother and had never really been loved by her mother. She had two siblings, a younger sister and a half-brother with a different father. Her grandmother had passed away but she still missed her every day. She still visited her grave occasionally to get in touch with her. Her half-brother was severely handicapped and she was more or less the only one who still visited him at the centre for the severely handicapped.

At some point she had been living together with her boyfriend and when the relationship ended she had tried to take her own life. That had been the second attempt. I felt moved by this story of a young woman living on the street, looking for warmth and affection. She had managed to survive in an environment like that by talking back and talking big. She had a friend that bossed her around and she let her because she really thought the friend cared about her. The only certainty life offered was her regular job at the health centre.

Her sad story got to me and I decided to help her. I talked to her about life and I tried to convince her that she should start believing in herself. I felt that she had a lot of warmth and love to give but that she did not know how to deal with it. There was always someone around taking advantage of her. I needed my God to be able to coach her and I also learned a great deal from her.

One thing I knew for sure, I could not give up on her. I sent her to different therapy sessions and sometimes they worked, sometimes they did not. It was never easy to get through to her yet slowly but surely she made progress and started to change her life around.

Sometimes there were these spells of silence but then she would call unexpectedly and we would meet. She smoked and needed the occasional joint she told me. Especially when she felt lonely she needed a joint. Another challenge presented itself because I wanted her to stop smoking pot. I had to help her and could not give up on her. It was what my God wanted and she was worth it. I had to teach her to love herself.

It was never easy though, and we often argued. She wanted to turn her life around and I wanted to help her at all costs. The horrible world she came from wanted her back and she had to fight her own battles. All I could do was offer advice. At the same time I could not suppress the feeling that she had not told me the full story and it seemed as if she did not know the full story herself.

I accompanied her on one of her visits to her handicapped brother and when I saw how full of love and caring she behaved towards him and how he appreciated it without being able to say so, I knew she was worth all my efforts towards helping her.

When she managed to buy a house and I was able to help her out with a mortgage it made me feel victorious. She was changing her life for the better step by step. I lent her some money (free of interest) to buy furniture and she was so enthusiastic about it all that it made me feel good.

In the meantime I had met a regression therapist who told me that she had been able to help people who had difficulties coming to terms with terrible experiences in the past. She was able to remove personal blockages that people suffered from. I sent my protégé to her and from this therapy she managed to derive the missing pieces of the jigsaw puzzle of her life.

Her father had raped her mother and which had led to her being born. As a result her mother had never been able to love her and her mother's ex-boyfriend had committed incest with my protégé and her sister. A horrible story and no wonder it had affected her. What could be worse? During the therapy sessions she was able to lift some of the blockades but all of a sudden she gave up on therapy. She had lost most of her anger by that time so it had been worth her while.

Six months later she told me she had taken part in a re-birthing session, which had made her feel at peace with herself and had enabled her to love herself again. In the meantime she was involved in a lasting relationship and the next time I met her I sat down opposite a wise and sensible women who had found balance in her life. She had wanted to overcome her past and be a winner. I was proud of her. We are still good friends and she calls me her angel.

I learned that helping others is not always easy. It is almost impossible to do so without getting emotionally involved. You need to feel a bond with the person if you are trying to help from the heart. Nevertheless, they still have to start by wanting to help themselves. Every relief worker needs to be patient. I once more appreciated my loving parents and my privileged surroundings.

The best way to bond with a customer is to do something for them. The customer will want to return the favour. The best relationships are based on reciprocity.

Cold calls and positive thinking

In my capacity of Country and CR manager[3] I was responsible for the sales process in the Netherlands. One of the company's objectives was to have one Standard Banking System in good working order in every country of the world. This had already been accomplished in 84 countries worldwide.

In order to reach that objective the Sales Director had decided that all aspiring salespeople had to attend 'cold call' training. I was also invited to attend and I subsequently left for the training location somewhere in a castle in the middle of nowhere.

The instructor was a friendly man and informed us that he was well familiar with our company and the product. He was a friend of one of the directors. What we did not know and what he did not tell us at the time was that he was to report afterwards to company management and was also to advise on who was suited to become a salesperson and who was not. There were eight of us and I was the oldest.

The first day we were instructed in the theoretical aspects of cold calls. How we were to behave, what we should say and what we should not say etc. etc. Very interesting and as we set down to work the instructor got to know us better through his interactive approach.

What we had not realised on the onset of the training became clear the next day. The instructor had a list with all banks and phone numbers in different countries. We were asked to call banks in our native countries. The official language was English so I had to try and make appointments with Dutch companies in the English language. The instructor listened in to our conversations and sometimes offered advice.

I managed to make appointments quite well because I benefitted from the drama training I had had as a youngster. The instructor was satisfied with my performance. He was particularly sensitive to body language and since I smiled and was cheerful he set my approach as an example to the others.

One of my colleagues was not doing too well and after about an hour she burst into tears. She had not managed to make one single appointment and it depressed her. She had told me the night before that due to personal

---

[3] Customer Relation Manager

circumstances she badly needed this job. I felt sorry for her and tried to help her whenever I could.

The instructor also tried to help her by means of giving her advice but it was not meant to be. She had not been able to make one single appointment and in the end she did not get the job.

I learned that studying the theoretical side of the matter is relatively simple. But to be able to put it into practice also depends and how you feel at that particular moment.

It's all sales

It is not fair on trainees not telling them that the instructor will also assess them. With this trick at the back of their minds they might behave differently during a next training session.

It could very well be possible that you are representing a good product at a good price and with excellent service. A prospect can nevertheless still say "no". Being turned down is never a pleasant experience. You may even think that you are not suited as a salesperson but bear in mind that the prospect might be experiencing personal problems. It could be the case that you called at the wrong moment. So it is not always your fault if the prospect is not interested. Nevertheless, even if you have the right basic attitude do not expect more than one positive response out of ten cold calls.

Selling under extreme pressure

The Sales Director of my company had been a successful salesperson for many years. He had done well for himself financially because he drove an impressive Porsche. He had been promoted to Sales Director and in my capacity of CR Manager (sales) I reported to him.

Once a month I would be invited to a sales meeting. I hated these meetings for they were badly organised and I liked well-run and efficient meetings. In the Netherlands office hours were from 9 a.m. to 5 p.m. One time I mentioned it and the others responded by saying, "well, you guys have to because you have dinner at 6". The Dutch were considered over organised! What fun all these cultural differences.

These sales meetings never started on time and most of the time the secretary had to chase salespeople throughout the entire building and shepherd them into the meeting room. Most salespeople would enter with their mobile phones glued to their ears. The Sales Director would be present as well and despite being in a meeting would be on the phone continuously. After about an hour one of the participants would usually say, "Why don't we get started?" And so after having wasted a full hour we could start the meeting.

All the Sales Director cared about was money. He hardly ever had a friendly word to spare for those on his team and put a lot of pressure on us if he something was in the pipeline. Sometimes he forced a salesperson to call a prospect on the spot and made the salesperson say to the prospect that he had to sign the contract that particular week. It was absolutely terrible and I could not help but notice that some of my colleagues lied about their prospects to the Sales Director in order to escape his wrath.

Given my experience in the finance industry in the Netherlands I knew that the bank managers were well educated and knew exactly what they were doing and when to decide. If a Dutch manager promised to call me he would. There was no need to force the matter. Dutch mangers did accept calls whenever they forgot to return a call. The only way to influence my prospect was by providing the right information and stick to my own promises. One call at the wrong moment could ruin the deal.

One of my prospects was on the brink of taking a decision and during the sales meeting the Sales Director forced me to call the prospect. Obviously I refused and told him why. You could have heard a pin drop in the meeting room while all those present were awaiting an outburst of anger from the Sales Director. This time he let me off the hook. He continued the meeting without saying anything about the matter. Somehow I could not escape the feeling that he did not like the way I had behaved.

I learned that if you put too much pressure on a prospect he might decide not to do business with you. You always have to stay in touch with your prospect and apply an acceptable amount of pressure.

It's all sales

As soon as a customer feels he is being pressured into taking a decision he will start wondering whether there are any problems. The insecurity will lead to postponing the decision. Of course it is not the same as leaving the customer to his own devices all together. It means that you always plan a new meeting with your customer. If the customer says, "I'll call you" your next question will be "when can I expect your call?" If you have not heard from the customer on that particular day it stands to reason that you will call the customer.

Selling as friends

As the Country and CR manager I was responsible for the sales of our product, a standard banking system, in the Netherlands. I was well aware of the competition but since I believed in our product I felt we could rely on our own strengths in the sales process. My objectives were to make sure that not only every bank knew what our product was all about but also to create awareness with every consultant in the country. Informing the consultants was important because in most cases the selection process was to be carried out by an external consultant in order to avoid conflicts of interest and safeguard an objective selection procedure.

The main managing consultancy company in the Netherlands had invited us to present our product to its banking consultants. I enjoyed giving presentations like these and accepted the invitation. After I had already accepted they told me that on the same night our main competitor was to give a presentation as well. Our competitor had indicated that they wanted my presentation to precede theirs and that they intended to be present. What could I do but express the desire to be present at their presentation. I had to accept their suggestion because we were the market leader in the Netherlands and their challenge was to beat us.

During my years of being employed in the finance industry I knew that the decision-making process with a bank was shrouded by company politics and that you could not hope to influence that process as a supplier. In the end the Board of Directors would base their decision on all the advice they had gathered. The only thing you could do as a supplier was to answer their RFIs and RFPs[4] to the best of your ability and make sure you lived up to the promises you made during the sales process. And above all, be kind, honest and considerate. The bottom line was that banks were highly capable of making their own decisions.

Another thing I had gathered from the many reference visits in the past was that banks were willing to believe that our software could perform in any way they wanted but what they feared was the actual implementation of the system. Therefore my presentations had mainly focussed on the implementation process. Still, the implementation process was an important part of all standard software, including that of the competition. As a result I decided to focus

---

[4] RFI = request for information and RFP = request for proposal

mainly on the extended functionality that was part of our product, one of our unique selling points when compared to the competition.

The presentation in itself was a success and the two directors of the competitor responded positively to my story. And I made jokes along the lines of "I think I taught you a thing or two" etc. It was an interactive presentation and a fun experience. Our competitor responded marvellously with lots of good-natured jokes about our story in their presentation that ultimately led to a pleasant and informative evening at which respect for each other was the key element.

That night the competitor's Sales Director and I became firm friends and after a deal we were in the habit of congratulating or consoling each other. We both knew that no matter how hard we tried, ultimately it was the customer who made the decisions. We never said anything negative about each other in the presence of a customer and we are still good friends to this very day.

I learned that as a salesperson you have to rely on the strengths of your own product. Never underestimate your customer and respect your competitors.

It's all sales

A salesperson should not only believe a full 100% in the product or service he sells, he has to identify with the product. You should be able to talk about your product with enthusiasm and show every one that your product or service is the best deal possible. It makes you feel in control and enables you to get a result as a matter of course.

Selling globally

For my current employer, a supplier of standard software to banks, I had as one of their first customers together with two other customers founded the global user group. Now that the number of customers had reached 400 the user group was changed into a Customer Forum to be organised annually at a unique location somewhere in Europe.

I liked taking part in these meetings. Most customers knew who I was and so did the managers and the colleagues. They were all business friends and I enjoyed their company.

Our charismatic Director was always prominently present and held one of his famous speeches. He regarded his customers, colleagues and employees as one big family. Usually the delegates from the Netherlands got together and we made sure we had a good time.

This Customer Forum proved to be a powerful sales instrument for the company. Banks were introduced to each other and made deals. Banks cooperated to define a new functionality. As a supplier it was relatively simple to introduce our new products and plans to everyone and we had easy access to the latest market developments. Whenever a prospect attended these sessions they were usually so impressed that they wanted to sign a contract on the spot.

Ever since this company had employed me I had also been invited by my colleagues to go to a disco. It had been quite a while since I had made any attempts at dancing but they talked me into it and much to my surprise I danced the night away. Most of my male colleagues were more interested in drinking but I was not. I spent the entire night on the dance floor and did not drink a drop of alcohol. I had always assumed that my daughter took after her mother because she loved to dance but it now became clear to me she must have inherited some dancing genes from me. I just let the music take part of me and I moved intuitively. Wow, what a feeling!

One of the Customer Forums took place at the French Riviera. I had arrived one day ahead and on that Saturday I walked along the boulevard in Nice. I saw the yachts passing by for it was obviously that time of year when the rich and famous showed off their wealth. I sat down on a bench and could not help but wonder whether these people were ever capable of experiencing a sense of freedom since they were almost all the time surrounded by staff and bodyguards. Not free and living in a golden cage. I felt joy at the feeling of freedom that surrounded me and I was grateful for the fact that I could do whatever I wanted.

I learned again that financial independence and emotional freedom made me happy. Meeting people from all over the world and different cultures offered a sense of liberation, which also made me experience a feeling of happiness.

Experiencing a sense of freedom means that you have no questions left to ask. True freedom can be found if you are able to do what you like doing and that you are able to deal with feelings like disappointment, other people's opinions and set backs and remain in touch with your own feelings. Stability is freedom. Freedom is being able to enjoy anything that comes you way. In order to achieve this, good self-analysis is essential. Sometimes you manage to do that all by yourself and sometimes you need help from others. As long as these others are honest with you. Getting help from a professional coach is not a sign of weakness, but rather a sign of strength.

Selling with a smile

As a Country and CR manager it was my job to maintain existing contacts and 'open the door' to other leads for my sales colleagues. Once the door was open, they could try and make a deal.

In my business plan I had included a comprehensive list of all the financial institutions in the Netherlands and I had sent them all an e-mail containing product and company information. In addition it was important to inform them that we were now able to offer support from a local affiliate.

It was simple really. We were already global market leader and every player in the market was aware of that. An independent trade journal published an annual list ranking the best-sold standard systems and we headed the list every year. Every consultant and every bank interested in purchasing a standard banking system consulted the list and sometimes we received a RFI or RFP without even visiting the bank.

The banking industry is a small world and no bank was willing to run unnecessary risks and wanted a banking system that had proven its worth in the market. Now that we had a local affiliate we could also offer local support (helpdesk), which was a major positive factor in a country where all bankers knew each other and shared their knowledge and experience.

One of my friends was a banker who was in the process of setting up an affiliate in the Netherlands for a foreign bank. He came to me with his business plan because he wanted to implement our software. He even went as far as to mention our company name in his business plan. I advised against this though, because of the neutral process that banks had to adhere to. I did not want his management to shoot down his proposal. He adjusted his business plan and his plan was eventually approved so he could start a neutral selection process.

My Sales Director was not pleased with the outcome of this story. But I was convinced we were going to win this deal because to me it was important that my friend remained neutral and as a result in charge of the Dutch affiliate of the bank.

This was a job I liked doing and I enjoyed meeting customers and prospects. I had also founded a national user group and all customers sent their representatives. This user group was an instant success and in only a short period of time we were already short-listed with three prospects. These were exciting times for the global sales team and me.

I learned that selling on behalf of a market leader is a piece of cake. Especially when existing customers are satisfied customers. The basis is trust and partnership. We had done a good job in establishing that.

Do not be mistaken. It will take a lot of effort before you hit the number one spot. Usually we only see the final results. An artist with a number 1 hit record, a painter with a masterpiece or a successful businessman. You cannot begin to guess at how many failed songs the singer recorded. How many preliminary sketches the painter produced or how many times the businessman missed out on an order. If you really want to achieve something you will have to work for it. That is why most people do not reach their goals. They never make it through the trial and error phase.

This is not my home

My daughter had been living on her own in the big city for a number of years. She lived in a small apartment that I had initially rented for her from one of my secretaries. Later on I had bought the apartment for her for tax purposes.

As a real student working her way through college she held a job in a perfumery every Thursday evening and Saturday and paid rent for the apartment to me. She called me every month to announce that she had transferred the rent money into my account. I invariably answered that she should take out a standing order. She still nursed the hope that I would tell her to skip that month's rent. Well, she was a clever girl my daughter, but her dad was even more clever. I do hope that does not still call the bank every month to let them know she paid the mortgage.

I had lived in the village where my daughter was born and raised for three years and as it turned out she had more friends in the big city where she now lived than in the village. Also she did no longer visit me at weekends as often as she did. So I decided the time had come for me to move to the big city as well, close to the office and close to my daughter. As a matter of coincidence, although I am not sure there is such a thing as coincidence, I managed to buy an apartment with a parking space close to the river in the big city. And by moving to the city of freedom I also took another step towards my own personal freedom.

Over the years my daughter had taken up the habit that whenever she visited me she would not lift a finger to clean up after her. I had talked to her about this annoying habit but she had answered that this was her home and that she automatically reverted to the old patter where I was to take care of her. It annoyed me also because whenever I visited her I had to take off my shoes at the front door in order not to soil her precious laminate flooring.

In the mean time I had moved to my new apartment in the big city that included a bath and a Turkish steam bath. My daughter thoroughly enjoyed those luxuries whenever she paid a visit and still did not clean up after her. It annoyed me and eventually she noticed it and left my house in an angry mood. Later on she called me and asked whether she could come round the next day, a Sunday, to talk things over.

It was difficult for me because we were good friends and she was no longer in touch with her mother. I did not want to be too hard on her or to hurt her unnecessarily. So when she arrived that Sunday I was friendly and cheerful. She sat down and told me that ever since I had moved into this new apartment she felt as if it was no longer her home.

I took it from there. I told her that it was not her home for her own house was her home now. Whenever I came to visit her I observed her house rules and I expected her to observe mine whenever she came to my house. She was no longer a student but an adult. We would also grant each other our privacy and call in advance. She understood and we parted as good friends and kept our promises.

I learned that being patient with children is important. Just wait for the right moment to make your point.

Also interpersonal processes take their time. Still, when pressure or irritation enters the equation it is important to raise the issue. If you do not, pressure will mount and will eventually manifest itself in a disproportionate manner and you will have a conflict on your hands. The best approach is to discuss the matter openly with those involved. Communicate with each other in a positive and critical manner. This approach also works with customers in a business environment.

Selling Customer Relation Management

The sales process of our product, the Standard Banking System, was a quite lengthy one and on some occasions it took years before the contract would be signed. It made sense because the implications for a bank were huge and it was important that all those involved were included in the decision-making process.

I had been employed as a Country and CR Manager[5] for this company and it was a job I enjoyed doing. I had been operating in the world of banking for many years and knew a considerable number of people and they knew me. I never saw myself as a real salesperson and in my opinion there was a large difference between a real salesperson and a customer relation manager. In my capacity of CR Manager I visited customers and could, when asked, open doors for the actual sales team. I also occasionally helped out the customer on other matters and sometimes even offered advice on personal matters. As far as I was concerned maintaining a good customer relationship was essential and I knew that because of all my efforts they would consider my company if they were ever going to buy standard software.

The actual salesperson visits the prospect with the sole aim of getting a result. He is willing to use every single argument he can think of to sell his product and can overstep the mark when making promises. A true salesperson never lies but does not always tell the whole truth either. He mostly tells the prospect what he wants to hear.

One of my colleagues was one of these super salespeople. He had been with the company for a number of years, was successful and had done well for himself. If he needed you he knew where to find you, if he did not need you, he could not be bothered talking to you.

He solely aimed at making deals and increasing his bonus. He was not exactly known for his intuition and sensibility. There were also some rumours concerning him and they had also come to my attention. It turned out that he was dating the charismatic Director's daughter.

I was curious though, and eager to watch him perform his magic. So when he invited me to a dinner with the directors of a prospect I jumped at the prospect of watching him at work. He had invited me to this dinner party because he had noticed that the directors who were to attend clearly liked me.

---

[5] Customer Relation Manager

The workshops for this prospect had already taken place and the directors now had to choose between two suppliers. They wanted to have dinner with us in the build-up to contract negotiations and to determine what the company was like as a supplier and a partner.

We entertained them lavishly at a top-notch restaurant and discussed at length the implementation of the banking system and likely problems. They wanted to hear from us how we could help them and they informed after past experiences with other banks.

My colleague focussed in his conversation on the successes of our company and the charismatic Director and his input. One moment he even told them that he was dating the charismatic Director's daughter in order to stress his own importance within the company. He added that the relationship was still a secret and nobody knew about it.

Well, you could have knocked me down with a feather because I never expected anything like this. He used his personal relationship as a sales tool. I could not believe it! I did notice that his remark did nothing to impress the prospect. The salesperson asked me afterwards to keep his secret.

I learned that in my opinion there is a rather large difference between a customer relation manager and a salesperson. Both are, none the less, essential in the sales process.

It's all sales

Previously we already stated that relationships are crucial to a salesperson. For is it not true that maintaining relationships is an essential part of the sales process? What happens if the salesperson in the story does not get the order? He will blame the CR Manager because it was obviously not a suitable prospect. The CR Manager will respond by saying that the salesperson did not use all the right sales arguments. The salesperson and CR manager could argue about this for a long time. Only a CR manager with excellent contacts and a well-maintained network can be successful. Salespeople do not lie but they are economical with the truth. A successful salesperson impresses customers and prospects with excellent results not by kissing the boss's daughter.

Partners in business

Another remarkable thing happened during the dinner with the prospect. One of the directors of the prospect insisted on paying the restaurant bill.

My colleague, who was the actual salesperson in charge, did not want to accept this generous offer but by means of signalling I managed to convince him that he had to accept, which is what he did in the end.

Our sales strategy was partly based on establishing a partner relationship with our customer. Our customer would be very dependent on our company after the implementation of the software system. For that reason they were not only interested in a supplier – customer relationship but also a partnership. They wanted to experience the feeling that we understood and solved their problems because we knew how important banking matters were. They wanted to be considered important.

During our walk back to the car my colleague was still very surprised. He did not understand because usually he was the one having to foot the bill. After all, we were the supplier. He was convinced that this would be the end of a prospective deal.

I explained to him that it was actually a very good sign. Dinner had been a relaxed and friendly affair and the Directors of the prospect had been pleased with the way our company had dealt with them. He had said so to me in the Dutch language. As a sign of their appreciation, and because they considered us equal partners they wanted to pay the bill. It was a positive sign.

The prospect signed the contract during the Customer Forum in the South of France to which I had not been invited. The salesperson had obviously already forgotten the important part I had played in the sales process.

I learned that people buy from people they like. If they like you, they will buy from you.

The most important aspect of a business relationship is the personal relationship. Customers are often heard saying that they want to keep business and private separate. Yet, also for these customers it is the personal relationship that will make the difference.

A top-notch dinner

Our charismatic Director was of Greek descent. He had purchased the Standard Software System for a few dollars and had sold it in about 90 countries to over 400 banks. His business acumen and marketing and sales instincts where phenomenal, for which he was widely respected. He was not a banker but he knew exactly what the banks expected from him and his company. His intention was never to lose out on a deal because of the price. If it did happen, he would get cross with the salesperson involved.

He worked incredibly hard and took pride in being able to tell everyone that he only needed four hours sleep a night. He was always on a plane going somewhere and if he summoned you to his present you had to make sure to get there as soon as possible, even in the middle of the night. He practically lived on black coffee alone and as far as he was concerned in business there were no time zones. He treated his company and customers as one big family. Unfortunately he did not always appreciate the fact that his friends and colleagues could not keep up with the accelerated growth of the company. Not every one who was knowledgeable about the standard system made a good manager. We called these developments 'teething troubles'.

We liked and respected each other and were always pleased to meet up. He appreciated my past efforts as a reference bank for his system and he had promised and given me a job for life.

Usually he joined negotiations at the final stages when the agreement was to be signed. The final points were left to him and were usually dealt with before a dinner to which the Directors of the prospect would be invited.

I had also been invited to one of those concluding dinners as had the salesperson and the pre sales team. The other diners taking part included the Board of Directors of the prospect. The negotiations had been concluded successfully so we could all sit back and enjoy an exquisite dinner in a star restaurant.

These dinners always served as stage for a 'performance' by the charismatic Director. He would entertain all those present by making jokes usually about his wife (the dragon lady) and the food. Because of his entertaining skills the atmosphere was always relaxed and because of him all these self-conscious bankers could unwind and relax. He was good at this and we all laughed and enjoyed ourselves.

When I drove him and my pre sales colleagues back to the hotel we were still happy because after all, a deal had been made. One of my pre sales colleagues said to the charismatic Director that it genuinely surprised him that he still had to laugh at the same jokes he had heard about a hundred times before. His remark made us start laughing all over again.

I learned that the charismatic Director made it abundantly clear to our prospect that he loved their company. He was honest and open and made them feel that they were equal partners. His jokes could break down barriers.

It's all sales

In the story above the right balance was struck. The way in which jokes and relaxation were used worked. However, the way in which it is done should suit you. Even if you do exactly what another person does in exactly the same words the results will not be the same. Never try to copy someone else. Do whatever suits you personally.

Not living up to your promises

My colleague was responsible for the Development and Maintenance Department in our company. In his other capacity of Account Manager he visited customers including some in the Netherlands. Eventually I was supposed to take over this part for the Netherlands and we were right in the middle of the transfer process. On account of this I visited a number of customers together with him.

He was a kind and clever fellow and he told me he had been a salesperson in the past and that his new role posed quite a challenge to him. It was not an easy job because most customers agreed that we had a good sales organisation but were not too happy with how the company lived up to its promises. Our delivery dates were not always met and we did not always stick to our planning. This would lead to having to draw up a new financial deal in order to solve the problems.

I was dumbfounded when I watched this kind Account Manager at work. He went to visit a customer and if the customer was dissatisfied and demanded immediate action he would call someone at the company and issue instructions in the presence of the customer to assign priority status to that particular customer and solve the problems.

The customer appeared satisfied but he did the same thing with every customer he visited. His colleagues were used to his approach by now and continued doing what they were doing in spite of his phone calls. Nothing ever happened and the customer accepted it. I simply could not believe it, but he got away with it.

They had deliberately separated the sales process from other processes within the company like maintenance and new developments. Sales staff was not to know about problems in other departments. All they had to do was sell. What happened after the deal was made was not their problem.

I learned that more is needed than just a good sales team to win. I would not and could not sell 'hot air. That kind of behaviour is unbefitting a good Customer Relation Manager.

The same thing goes for every company. Dealing with customers is a continuous process. One person is responsible and all the other departments serve to support the customer. A salesperson (account manager) is responsible for dealing with every customer aspect and needs to make sure that everything is done to serve the interests of the customer.

Selling without a deal

One day the Director-general of one of my customers called me in a state of anger. He was not angry with me but with my colleague, the head of the Maintenance and Development Department. He did not beat about the bush when he expressed his opinion about my supposedly nice colleague. The colleague had visited the customer and had been forced to admit that a new software module that had to be developed especially for the customer was still not finished. Even worse, they had not even started work on the software module. The Director-general had every reason to be upset because he also told me that he could not introduce his new product to the market and was therefore missing out on a considerable amount of money. He was so angry that he had decided to contact his solicitor to sue for damages.

Company management had been changed in anticipation of the stock market flotation and a friend of our charismatic Director (also a Greek) had been appointed company comptroller. With his appointment he became second in control. I had already met this new comptroller on one previous occasion and it did not take me long to find out that that he had an excellent head for figures but had no clue as to what kind of business we were in and knew nothing about our customers, the banks. It reminded me of problems I had had in the past with comptrollers.

He came to the Netherlands to pay a visit to the dissatisfied customer. He never discussed the matter beforehand with me nor with my colleague, who had caused the problem. Once the meeting was over he left on a plane straight away without informing me. I was, of course, dying to find out what had been discussed, for after all it was my customer. So I decided to send the comptroller an e-mail to carefully inquire after the outcome of the meeting.

He answered that he had made a financial deal with the customer. The customer was to get the software module free of charge within six months time. This was a firm delivery date. I did not understand because nothing had been conceded on the customer's part. The customer had not even promised to withdraw their claim for damages. This had nothing to do with a deal, this was a give-away. I knew from experience that this customer was in the habit of running rings around us.

The comptroller had made the deal without asking for anything in return. I sent him a reply asking what the customer had promised to do in return for this favourable deal. I never received a reply and the comptroller avoided me whenever I ran in to him.

Next, I called the customer's Director-general and he told me that he had arranged that my colleague, who had caused the problem, was never to set one foot in his building again. He felt dependent on us, the supplier, and had no other choice but continue doing business with us.

I pretended I was well informed about the deal and I promised I would protect his interests to the best of my ability. I also asked him not to inform other banks about the deal and he said he would not.

I learned that a supplier could abuse his position of strength with a customer, secure in the knowledge that the customer depends on him. But in the end it will cost a lot of money and it will lead to losing customers.

It's all sales

Despite the fact that mistakes are being made by a company it does not mean that you give everything away. We know that it even makes the customer feeling uncomfortable. The comptroller chose the line of least resistance. Doing something like this has nothing to do with the sales process. Giving something for free is simple. Selling only starts when the customer has objections or says 'no'. Then it is up to the salesperson to listen to the customer and work together to come up with a suitable solution. The outcome can never be one-sided but both parties have to benefit from it.

The truth does not sell

Company policy regarding the sales process and local affiliates had been altered. The local sales and pre sales staff no longer reported to the country managers but directly to the Sales Director. More sales staff had been taken on and a new female salesperson was appointed for the Netherlands, my home country and the country I had been responsible for as Country and CR Manager. I had not been involved in the recruitment process and all I could do was hope I would be able to cooperate with her. I had been able to work together with her predecessor and I hoped we could continue business as before.

I accepted my new role in the scheme of things and gave her my trust. I also provided her with all the information about the prospects in the Netherlands and I explained to her my position of CR manager and invited her to make use of my contacts. She could benefit from my knowledge and experience and by doing so add to her own bonus. I was under the impression that she did not want to listen because she only ever responded by asking that since I was so knowledgeable why I had not been appointed salesperson. Was I after her job? She never asked for help and was convinced she could do it all by herself. I did not feel right but I could not force her to cooperate with me.

In that period of time one of our prospects was about to make a decision in their selection process. I had helped the Director-general with his business plan and it seemed we were going to secure the deal. The new sales woman had taken over this customer and it looked as if she was to land a safe first deal.

Unfortunately the automation specialists of the mother bank were creating problems and demanded that our Standard Banking System would be available on their platform of choice, including the database. Our eager sales team had of course promised that this was feasible but we had no experience with their automation environment. We also lacked a production environment for their database of choice since this was still in a test phase.

We were on the brink of the actual closing of the deal with this prospect. They were to choose between our main competitor and us and we were close in terms of proposal and solutions. All of a sudden the saleswoman received an internal e-mail stating that many problems had arisen during the testing of the database. Without giving it any thought and without asking for advice, the sales woman forwarded the message directly to the customer. It goes without saying that we lost the deal. The customer no longer trusted us.

I learned that she was simply too honest with the customer. Automation problems can almost always be solved. Sometimes being too honest can drive a customer away. A deal is only finite once the contract is signed.

In sales it is important that you can trust each other. This is also the basis of solid partnership. If you really cannot live up to a customer's expectations you have to admit to it but at the same time come up with alternatives. You can also ask yourself the question how essential this customer demand is. Sometimes it is the turn of phrase that makes the difference. In some cases something seems more important to a customer than it really is. You cannot lose out on a deal because of that.

Mediation as a tool

My previous employer had organised mediation training courses for all the interim managers and project managers. I had missed out on these sessions because I had already left the company after six months. Still, after having listened to the experiences of those who had been on the course I was interested and when my manager indicated that I was allowed to go on a training course I immediately jumped at the opportunity to go on a mediation training course. I thought it might improve my managerial skills. Management approved my plan and I enrolled for this course that was to be divided into three blocks of two days each.

A mediator is someone who solves conflict situations and problems in an impartial manner by means of asking questions and above all by having participants come up with possible solutions without letting personal emotions get in the way. I was someone who took decisions quickly and now they were teaching me methods not to take decisions but letting others do it themselves. I enjoyed this training course because it involved lots of practice sessions in workshops and I enjoyed playing parts. On completion of the course I was an official mediator.

In the Netherlands everyone could set him or herself up as a mediator. Once you had finished your training you could register as a mediator with the Dutch Mediation Institute. Slowly but surely more attention was given to the business of mediation because an increasing number of judges had started reverting cases to a mediator instead of a solicitor.

During the training sessions I had met three fellow mediators all living in the same big city. We thought it would be a good idea to team up and stay in touch to exchange knowledge and experiences. We decided to set up and exploit a joint website. We all four came from different backgrounds and would be able to offer custom-made service to a potential customers. Next to that, most customers were not too keen on doing business with a sole enterprise. In this set up they could choose between four mediators.

I had enjoyed this training course and I felt it had done wonders for me. It enabled me to advise my younger colleagues in an impartial way and I was better equipped to deal with their emotions. Also as a CR Manager it served its purpose to be able to ask open questions and not take over the conversation too fast.

Many of those around me had told me on occasion that I was not the world's greatest listener. And I had to admit listening was not one of my best features. Still, not listening had enabled me to reach my goals. Sometimes people do not

226

want you to listen but to do exactly as they say and that is something completely different. I had to learn to listen, though, and as a mediator I was forced to do just that. And it was good for me I had to admit.

I learned that I never wanted to stop learning. Learning something new made feel enthusiastic and creative time and again. For me this was a continuous process.

It's all sales

In sales most people have the tendency to stick to a well-tried working order. In order to continue successfully it is essential that you keep looking for improvements. During your search you will come across new information that you can use to make your visits more exciting for your customers. This also relates to information that might at a first glance have nothing to do with sales but could contribute to a better relationship with your customer.

No sex means not selling

In my working life I have always had a number of principles I stuck to. One of those principles was to never get involved with a woman from work. All the women in my working environment knew this and it made them feel secure with me. There were of course firm friendships with female colleagues but I think just being friends added to the quality of the friendship.

There were two reasons why I stuck to my principles. First of all, because my mother's role had always been important in my family. My parents had been equal but there always had been a strict division of tasks. Because of the way I was raised I respected women and I treated them as equals. The second reason was that with a previous employer I had watched a Director (with a picture of his wife and family on his desk) getting involved in a relationship with his secretary. The affair had led to his dismissal and their behaviour had annoyed me immensely.

Within our company there was a natural division between employees in the North of Europe and the South. On a personal level it did not bother me but at some point I was confronted with this division in a negative way. We had made a major deal with a bank in the Netherlands. It had been decided that a woman from Southern Europe would manage the project and she had only assigned people from the South to this project.

I was just itching to get my hands on the project but I was never considered for the job and local staff was never called in. As a Country Manager I thought this was wrong, especially given the inevitable language problems and local staff would be perfectly capable of applying their knowledge, and experience to this project.

I had known the Project Manager for quite a while. She had been with the firm for a long time and was part of the 'family". She had been involved in several affairs with colleagues and she had told me on occasion that because of her travels she had lost touch with most of her friends at home.

Her colleagues were now her friends. This situation was not good for her reputation though, because her behaviour got a lot of bad press. She knew how to use her femininity to reach her goals.

I had sent her an e-mail to explain that I was not pleased with her outline of the project. From her response it became clear that she was well aware of the fact that I was quite close to the charismatic company Director. She suggested that we should meet and discuss the matter during the international sales meeting that had been planned for the following week.

The night of the sales meeting she came to see me after dinner and asked me to meet her late that night in the hotel bar. I looked her into the eyes and noticed that she had quite something else on her mind. This feeling was reinforced by her sexy behaviour. One of my colleagues who had witnessed it all even made a very relevant remark about it.

I met her later that night in the bar and behaved as formally as I could. She promised she would adjust the project organisation and would use my and my local staff's expertise. During the conversation she more or less tried to seduce me. She was wearing this very sexy outfit but I pretended not to notice. I told her I was tired and that it was time for me to retire and I paid the bill. I gathered from the look on her face that this was not according to plan and that she was angry with me for not being susceptible to her charms.

The result of the matter was that nothing in the project changed and it was never finished successfully.

I learned that living up to your own principles is not always good for the company. It is good for you, though.

It's all sales

As a salesperson you sometimes end up in situations like this. It is of course flattering that someone is willing to go all the way to humour you. There are of course principles you have to stick to. Nevertheless, if somebody is ready and willing to go this far to reach goals from which you will also benefit, why stop them completely. Without compromising your integrity you can try to humour this person in a creative way and not compromise the working relationship.

No knowledge does not sell

This bank was a midsize private Bank in the Netherlands. They had initiated a new selection process to replace their self-built systems by a standard banking system. I had known this company and its management for several years and I knew that a couple of years before they had tried, albeit unsuccessfully, to implement a standard system. This bank took up a lot of a supplier's time and was known for its slow decision-making process. They had already 'got through' a number of Automation Managers. We were careful not to spend too much time on this bank.

Things had changed for the better though, and the bank had hired a new Automation Manager with a strong personality. He was change-driven and since I had worked with him in the past I knew what he was capable of. We respected each other.

My colleague, the recently appointed saleswoman, had taken over this customer from me. She had asked me to introduce her but had not invited me to the meeting. She was still convinced I was after her job while by now she should have known better. If she had, she would have made use of my expertise and contacts and in doing so increase her bonus.

I did not know when she was due to visit the bank but one afternoon my phone rang and my contact called me and told me that he had thought it strange that only the saleswoman had paid him a visit that morning.

He had not at all been pleased with her visit because she had not been able to answer a single one of his questions. She had to get back to him on almost every issue and just did not have a clue. He got slightly angry with me and asked me whether I had sent her over for sex. He finally made it clear to me that he did not want her to visit him again and wanted to do business with me.

I now had a problem on my hands because I knew that this new saleswomen was supported by the Sales Director. He had recruited her and probably told her to visit customers on her own. In addition I had noticed that he was quite impressed by the saleswoman's feminine charms. She and a member of the pre sales team had the Sales Director's ear and they were no friends of mine. I decided to let the company's and the prospect's interests prevail.

When the Sales Director paid us a visit I told him in a businesslike fashion what the prospect had conveyed to me. He did not like what he heard for now he also had a problem on his hands. He was not a real manager but was always keen on increasing his bonus and was definitely interested in bringing in this customer.

My new colleague had already lost out on a deal by forwarding the wrong e-mail to a customer so he did not appreciate her sales track record so far. At the end of our conversation he reproached me for not having given her a chance to be successful in the Netherlands. I looked at him and knew it was not true. Unfortunately at that point in time I was the only one who believed that.

I learned again that people buy from people. It is always about human interaction. I did feel upset by the allegations made by the Sales Director because they were absolutely not justified.

It's all sales

People buy from people. Sometimes it is interesting to see that a customer only buys from a certain company because it is where you work and you are his contact. The danger is evident; the company depends heavily on you. In many companies company hierarchy reinforces authority. A real manager knows how to value his people and how to stimulate them so they will not pose a threat to the company's continuity but are an asset.

The 'dancing queen'

This year the Customer Forum had been situated in a beautiful hotel on the French Riviera. It was once again a spectacular location and almost every customer was present. It was a wonderful event especially because this time would be the first time I was to take part in my capacity of Country Manager. For my friends, the Dutch customers, it did not make a difference. We were still the same and had a lot of fun together.

Like every year the main event of the gathering was a formal dinner organised by my employer, the supplier. This time it was a dinner dance and a cover band played all the songs by the famous British pop group Queen. The music was great and although all those present were familiar with the songs not a lot of dancing was going on. That made sense because although the music was good it was not exactly suited for dancing. I assumed that some more alcoholic beverages needed to be served before those brave enough dared to take to the dance floor.

This year's event was also special because of the presence of one of my prospects. This was a first for me but I was almost sure that this prospect would sign the contract once the event was over. The family feeling would in the end convince them, I was certain of it. Their Automation Manager, a nice lady, headed the team of the prospects. We got along well.

I always made sure that the Dutch customers would be seated at the same table. We had one goal and that was not to 'talk shop'. We were out there to enjoy the food, the wine and ourselves. The great atmosphere at the Dutch table had already gained a reputation among the other delegates. The prospect's delegation was also seated at the Dutch table and joined in the fun. The Automation Manager was seated next to me.

Once I left the table for a short while my foreign colleagues approached me and felt the urge to make obscene jokes and told me tonight was the night and I had to get them to sign the contract. Lots of fun for the others and in particular for those seated at the sales table.

In actual fact the music was a problem because nobody was dancing, and the thought of dancing never crossed my mind. The music was too 'difficult' to dance to and I was not brave enough to be the first to take to the dance floor.

Unfortunately my table-companion, our prospect's Automation Manager, thought otherwise and after a couple of glasses of red wine she asked me to dance. There was no way I could have turned her down. There was a deal at stake. I was horrified but I had to join her on the dance floor.

Amidst loud cheers and many 'funny' remarks I walked with her to the dance floor and did my duty. She obviously enjoyed herself. We were the only ones on the dance floor and about 400 guests were looking at us. I could feel their eyes burning in my back and tried my best to make the most of it.

For months after the Customer Forum my colleagues addressed me as the 'Dancing Queen'.

I learned that it is important to entertain your prospects and show them a good time. It will make them feel a part of the family. One thing though, never get drunk.

It's all sales

It is very useful to organise an annual customer event. You will meet your customers in a different setting. You will see that the behaviour of those present will change. It is important that your customers and prospects have a good time and can enjoy themselves. It is also important to make them feel important and respected. What could be more fun and challenging than to have a prospect or customer asking you to dance? Do not mind your colleagues. They are just jealous. You are dancing with a 'contract' and they are not. It is the best way to be successful. Dance with them (you make the same movements and experience the same rhythm).

Business and private friends

My life had changed once more and sometimes I felt incredibly lonely. I was no longer in charge of the sales staff. The position of Country Manager had not been defined properly and I felt they only treated me correctly because I was close to the charismatic company Director. I felt useless and I still went through the motions but I missed having a real challenge.

I had written a business plan for the Dutch affiliate but when it was to be presented to the new Board of Directors, the new Directors were not interested and left for another meeting. My presentation was skipped while others were offered the opportunity to present theirs. A Country Manager was apparently not important enough. Without a real challenge or project to sink my teeth into I get bored and I become a nuisance and in particular to myself.

There were thirteen of us employed at the Dutch affiliate. Most of them were my friends and had worked for me before. Only the saleswoman and the pre sales employee did not report to me. I only had to create facilities for them. They both did not accept my position of CR manager, which made it difficult for me because that is what I was good at.

This time I had made the mistake of mixing business with private because I was alone at home and also because I was engaged in haptonomy sessions and felt insecure about my behaviour. In the end it was all for the best but I was still in the middle of the process I had to get through. At that point I felt there was not a lot to like about myself. I was once more looking for stability in my life and I was also hypersensitive and easily upset. I expected too much in return from those I had helped which of course did not happen, but I felt now was as good time as any to learn to receive.

I had known one of my female colleagues for many years. We had been through a lot together and she was married to my best friend. She earned good money and since her husband wanted to put in fewer hours it simply meant she had to work harder. I met my best friend on a regular basis but it struck me that he did not really know what he wanted from life. We discussed it often, to little result.

She came to see me unexpectedly and told me she was to resign. I was surprised and I could not escape the feeling that the reason she gave for her resignation was not the real reason. Her husband, my best friend, never contacted me again. That caused a lot of pain. I still see her regularly but I feel there is this secret between us. Regrettable because I felt I had lost two friends.

At the end of each month my colleagues went out to dinner and would have a few drinks beforehand, this to tighten the bond. Most employees were with customers most of the time so these monthly dinners proved an opportunity for us to meet. One day after lunch I fell ill. I had contracted a serious case of food poisoning and dinner or no dinner I had to take a taxi home. I was too ill to take part.

All my employees were aware of this because they had watched me taking off in a taxi. Things got worse once I arrived home and I was sick to the bone. I was in bed with a high fever.

I had to stay in bed till the next day when I felt slightly better. Not one of my colleagues had contacted me to ask how I was doing. People I had known for years who I had always helped and supported could not be bothered to pick up the phone to ask how I was doing. I was downright disappointed but told myself not to expect too much. It all became clear to me now. I had to change my life.

I learned that I once again I needed to keep business and private separate. In the past I had been able to do this but for some reason I had forgotten this golden rule. And I had to learn to give without expecting something in return. God will give what you deserve but never when you expect it and in His own way.

It's all sales

Having friends, real friends, is something special. It is the feeling of sharing something with someone else that makes it special. Yet, sometimes there are feelings that resemble friendship and these feelings may lead to calling many people a friend. Being able to work together well and staying in touch does not make you friends. As soon as the common denominator, work, disappears it will become apparent what the contact was worth.

Bad management and no deal

This company had employed me for three years as a Country Manager. I earned a good salary and the benefits included a bonds scheme for the employees. Every year the charismatic Director rewarded me with extra bonds as a sign of his appreciation for my past work for the company. Many colleagues owned a considerable amount of these bonds and everybody was eagerly awaiting the stock market flotation. That would enable them to cash in on their bonds. Many colleagues were no longer happy working for the company. The company expanded rapidly which made it difficult for them to do business and new managers were appointed and disappeared at the drop of a hat.

The stock market floatation brought about certain measures including a cutback in expenditure. The new comptroller, the second in command, had been crossing FTEs[6] off a spreadsheet which meant forced redundancies.

The ones who were to be fired were not the ones with the large amount of bonds but the newcomers. My fifth manager in three years time called me to say that he was to pay me a visit the next day and that he would be accompanied by the HR manager.

I was wondering what he wanted from me but since both were new to the company, I assumed it would be a courtesy call. Well, that was not the case because as soon as the pair of them had arrived the Manager made it clear to me that I had to fire three employees on the spot. He had the names of the unfortunate ones written on a piece of paper. He asked me to call them into my office so the HR Manager could fire them immediately.

That was the absolute limit. They had not consulted me about this beforehand. This was a surprise attack. These people were my friends and I had asked them to leave their previous employers to come and work for us. We were engaged in two new projects so there was plenty of work. I stayed calm and explained to my manager that was not the way things worked in the Netherlands. My employees would take the matter to court and given the good financial position of the Dutch affiliate this was going to cost the company a great deal of money. I asked my manager for permission to consult directly with the charismatic Director and comptroller via e-mail and forward the message to him as well. In this way the manager would stay out of range. He gave me permission and told the HR Manager to return to the head office.

---

[6] FTE = Full Time Equivalent. 1 FTE = one full time worker

Another one of their demands was that I had to become billable for two days a week. In addition to my work as Country Manager I would also be employed as a consultant. I did not raise this issue with my manager that afternoon for it was not important at the time. My staff's best interests were what mattered.

That night sent my e-mail with arguments to both directors. My advice was not to fire people in the Netherlands because we were doing quite well, but to examine other options to cut back expenditure. I wrote that I understood measures needed to be taken for the good of the company but that firing these people would lead to severe financial consequences.

The charismatic Director, my friend, never responded to my e-mail. The comptroller did though, and he responded by telling me that I should not leave the company but that I had to fire the three employees. He added that it was essential to have sufficient staff for local customer support. Two lines before that he had just summoned me to fire exactly those employees. It was beyond me and it hurt.

It was a cruel awakening. I told the three employees about the managerial decision with pain in my heart. Fortunately they understood and they took it with grace. Naturally they took the company to court and were awarded some money. I also helped them to find another job. It was the only thing left for me to do.

Now the time had come to make up my own mind. Management ignored me completely and did not consult me before making a decision. I was not appreciated for my knowledge but because I had been a friend of the boss who had promised me a job for life. That was not what I was all about. If you allow people to trample all over you it will be the beginning of the end. It was too much for me to put up with and I decided to resign and look for another challenge.

Still, my God was good to me, because two days later a head-hunter contacted me and told me that given my successful position in the market a supplier of standard software packages for banks was interested in employing me. The job on offer was that of CR Manager and Account Manager for a number of European Countries. I had to build local affiliates from scratch. The new challenge had presented itself just in the nick of time.

I resigned and kept believing in my principles even if it meant not becoming a bond millionaire.

I learned that everything in my life happened at the right moment. I just had to rely on my God and He would take care of me. I felt rich beyond money.

Also in management teams you will find normal people with their own personal skills and limitations. Sometimes important decisions are taken in a clumsy way. Often based on a hierarchical structure lacking the support of those involved. The result is frustrations that will lead to a decrease in productivity and commitment. It is always difficult to communicate a policy of change.

Selling a new start to myself

After a number of 'readings' it had become clear to me. I should follow the road to freedom: financial and emotional freedom. I was now living in the city of freedom where everyone could be whoever and whatever he or she wanted to be. I had a new job and a new challenge. The only thing holding me back was the high monthly alimony I still had to pay to my ex-wife. I had discovered a lot about myself during a difficult process. I was ready for a new start.

I was a 'rich' man and I based that conviction on all the lessons I had been forced to learn the hard way. Naturally I did miss having a partner, a woman to love and love me. The best part of life is a cherished partner. I was convinced of that. Regrettably that blank in my life had not been filled as yet but in spite of that I felt happy and most of all free. I read a lot, listened to my music, played indoor-soccer and badminton and I met many, many people because I spent a lot of time travelling. Every time I went on a business trip it felt like going on holiday. When I was on the road I no longer had to think about food, laundry, housekeeping etc. I just left the house and closed the door behind me, a new adventure awaiting me.

In this job I was a manager without staff. I could start from scratch and all I had to do was find new customers for their standard banking systems. Once customers were found we could start building an organisation around them.

An acquaintance of mine gave therapy sessions based on NLP[7]. She gave me a number of statements I had to repeat to myself every day. In doing so I would start loving myself more. In fact, I was reprogramming myself.

I had started with the sessions but they made me think and I stopped. The whole process scared me. All I wanted was to be myself. And if that meant I was a giver, so be it. Wanting to give to others was something worthwhile. I felt good about myself. NLP was a method that when used by the wrong people could lead to major problems.

So looking back at my life up till then I could conclude that I had mainly been motivated by earning money followed by having power and thirdly enjoying life every single day. I was also able to add to that knowledge and life experience.

My God had made it all possible for me and had introduced me to the right people in my life. I had been allowed to perform miracles. Now I had to put my

---

[7] Neuro Linguistic Programming

trust in Him and let things happen. If I managed to do so, living my life would me more quiet and simple. I thanked Him every night for allowing me to lead a life as a true human being.

All the lessons I had learned had made me who I was. A good basis to continue with renewed courage and make a fresh start.

Being yourself is what is most important in life. Whether it is a God who helps you or whether it is a kind of energy you generate yourself that enables you to reach our goals, it does not matter. As long as it touches upon what makes you happy. What is your reason for being?

Index

Business

Market

Family matters